Taking Teaching Seriously:
Meeting the Challenge of Instructional Improvement

by Michael B. Paulsen and Kenneth A. Feldman

ASHE-ERIC Higher Education Report 2, 1995

Prepared by

*Clearinghouse on Higher Education
The George Washington University*

In cooperation with

*Association for the Study
of Higher Education*

Published by

*Graduate School of Education and Human Development
The George Washington University*

Jonathan D. Fife, Series Editor

Cite as
Paulsen, Michael B., and Kenneth A. Feldman. 1995. *Taking Teaching Seriously: Meeting the Challenge of Instructional Improvement.* ASHE-ERIC Higher Education Report No. 2. Washington, D.C.: The George Washington University, Graduate School of Education and Human Development.

Library of Congress Catalog Card Number 96-76558
ISSN 0884-0040
ISBN 1-878380-66-4

Managing Editor: Lynne J. Scott
Manuscript Editor: Barbara Fishel, Editech
Cover design by Michael David Brown, Rockville, Maryland

The ERIC Clearinghouse on Higher Educaton invites individuals to submit proposals for writing monographs for the *ASHE-ERIC Higher Education Report* series. Proposals must include:
1. A detailed manuscript proposal of not more than five pages.
2. A chapter-by-chapter outline.
3. A 75-word summary to be used by several review committees for the initial screening and rating of each proposal.
4. A vita and a writing sample.

ERIC Clearinghouse on Higher Education
Graduate School of Education and Human Development
The George Washington University
One Dupont Circle, Suite 630
Washington, DC 20036-1183

This publication was prepared partially with funding from the Office of Education Research and Improvement, U.S. Department of Education, under contract no. ED RR-93-002008. The opinions expressed in this report do not necessarily reflect the positions or policies of OERI or the Department.

EXECUTIVE SUMMARY

"Taking Teaching Seriously" is drawn from a celebrated address by K. Patricia Cross at the 1986 AAHE National Conference on Higher Education in Washington, D.C. In her address, Cross emphasized the importance of efforts to increase the quality of college teaching. This report uses a model that views various strategies for improving instruction as helping motivate individual faculty members to improve their teaching by changing (and maintaining) certain of their instructional attitudes and practices (through the process of unfreezing, changing, and refreezing certain attitudes and behaviors). This model focuses on the varieties of informative feedback—from such sources as colleagues and consultants, chairs, students, and oneself—that are facilitated by a supportive teaching culture and that drive the process of instructional improvement.

What Are the Primary Characteristics of a Supportive Teaching Culture?

The presence of a culture that is supportive of teaching clearly enhances the effectiveness of all strategies for improving instruction. The literature consistently identifies the following characteristics of cultures that support teaching and its improvement: unambiguous commitment to and support of teaching and its improvement from senior administrators; shared values about the importance of teaching between administrators and faculty, with widespread involvement of faculty in planning and implementing activities and programs to improve teaching, thus creating a sense of faculty "ownership" of these activities and programs; the presence of effective department chairs who are supportive of teaching and its improvement; frequent interaction and collaboration among faculty and a sense of community among faculty regarding teaching-related issues; a faculty development program or campus teaching center; a broad, expanded view of scholarship and scholarly activities; decisions about tenure and promotion connected to rigorous evaluations of teaching; and a requirement that some demonstration of effective teaching be part of interviewing and hiring new faculty (Massy, Wilger, and Colbeck 1994; Rice and Austin 1990).

What Strategies to Improve Instruction Help Teachers Provide Informative Feedback to Themselves?

Because college teachers often have a strong need to seek self-determined competence by continuously scanning the instructional environment for informative feedback, their behavior can be examined and the source of changes in their behavior understood by viewing them as "reflective practitioners." Activities that constitute such practice-centered inquiry have been shown to be useful strategies for improving instruction (Amundsen, Gryspeerdt, and Moxness 1993). The ultimate foundation of all reflective practice or self-reflection is the ability and opportunity to engage in self-evaluation or self-assessment. Two common methods of collecting self-evaluation feedback at universities involve the use of self-rating forms and self-reports. At some colleges and universities, for example, faculty are asked to complete the same (or slightly reworded) questionnaires to evaluate teaching as their students. This procedure enables faculty to analyze their teaching and to reflect on their teaching behaviors along the same dimensions their students use to evaluate them. A second method, self-reports completed by college professors, has traditionally been limited to vitae and reports of activities; recently, however, the idea of self-reports has been conceptually and functionally expanded into a medium, compendium, and showcase for reflective practice—namely, the teaching portfolio, which is essentially an elaborate and reflective form of self-evaluation (Edgerton, Hutchings, and Quinlan 1991).

How Can Students Make Their Voices Heard?

Students hardly need to be "silent partners" in the enterprise of improving teaching. One way their voices can be heard is through their completing teacher and course evaluations. Research has shown persistently that feedback from student ratings is of value in improving teaching, particularly if this feedback is accompanied by the teacher's consulting with a colleague or a teaching consultant (L'Hommedieu, Menges, and Brinko 1990). Several different ways of using student interviews for giving feedback to teachers have also been reported as successful strategies for improving instruction, including group discussions, small-group instructional diagnosis, the class interview, and quality-control circles. A particularly distinctive way of receiving feedback from students is for a professor to invite students into his or her classroom who are not "official" members of the class but who are trained in classroom observation. A student-visitor program primarily provides confidential observations to increase the instructor's effectiveness in helping students learn. Another strategy for "listening" to students has been called "classroom assessment," which consists of a wide range of methods college teachers can use to obtain useful feedback on what, how much, and how well their students are learning (Angelo and Cross 1993).

How Can Colleagues, Consultants, and Chairs Be Helpful in Improving Teaching?

Faculty seminars, workshops, and colloquia about teaching are traditional (but still effective) practices for encouraging interaction and collaboration among faculty regarding teaching. Recent developments in a variety of areas—action science, reflective practice, adult learning theory, and the like—have encouraged an expanded range of strategies using colleagues to help improve teaching. One important set of activities, programs, and projects in this expansion is the renewed use of team teaching (Baldwin and Austin 1995). Faculty collaboration through team teaching benefits professors by developing their teaching abilities, intellectually stimulating them, engaging them as self-directed learners, and more closely connecting them to the university or college as a community. A second set of programs and practices is collegial coaching (Keig and Waggoner 1994). Two primary activities involved in collegial coaching are observation of classroom teaching and instructional consultation (the review of course materials and discussions about classroom practices). Based on descriptions and analyses of coaching projects at colleges and universities, effective programs have all or most of the following characteristics: an underlying philosophy; a procedure for selecting participants; a training program for collegial coaches; a preobservation conference; one or more classroom visits and observations; a postobservation conference; and a chance for participants to evaluate their effectiveness.

Many of the informal processes of consultation carried out in collegial coaching projects have been formalized in a comprehensive set of more routine services provided by the trained consultants who constitute the staff of campus teaching centers. Instructional consultation is usually based on a comprehensive model that includes data collection and analysis by the consultant, strategies for improvement worked out between the consultant and the teacher, and evaluation (Lewis and Povlacs 1988). Consultation improves teaching primarily through the use of effective practices in giving feedback (often associated with student ratings and direct observation or videotapes of classroom teaching) and through the various interpersonal roles assumed by consultants.

Department chairs are also important to the improvement of teaching. One way they help is by providing support—financial and otherwise—to ongoing formal and informal attempts to improve teaching. They are invaluable in defining faculty development and instructional improvement (as distinct from faculty evaluation) as an important departmental activity. They can plan programs for the department, such as pedagogical colloquia, that help improve teaching. They can even intervene more directly by following steps similar to those used in instructional consultation (Creswell, Wheeler, Seagren, Egly, and Beyer 1990).

How Can the Special Needs for Improving the Teaching of New and Junior Faculty Be Met?

Because new faculty members share common concerns about such matters as workload and stress from multiple demands, uncertainty about what is expected of them, a desire for collegial support, and a need to develop teaching skills, a strong argument can be made for supplementing traditional, individual approaches of socialization that help them adjust to their new environment with a collective approach that address these common concerns. Workshops and "substantial" orientation programs for new faculty members that offer concrete assistance with the development of teaching skills and with various common problems are being used successfully in a variety of colleges and universities. In addition, formal mentoring programs for new and junior faculty are also being used at different schools to give concrete assistance with the development of teaching skills, to address professional and personal concerns, and, in general, to counter the vagaries of the usually informal socialization of new college teachers (Boice 1992b; Sorcinelli and Austin 1992).

What Can Colleges Do to Improve Teaching?

Several approaches, used in concert, can be used to improve instruction in colleges and universities. Ways need to be found to "unfreeze" certain attitudes and behaviors of some teachers that prevent them from improving their teaching. Supportive teaching cultures on campus must be strengthened, especially at those colleges where such cultures are subsidiary to more dominant cultures. More teachers need to be given guided experience in being "reflective practitioners." Students should be treated (and sought out) as active partners in the improvement of instruction. Formal and informal collaboration among colleagues should be rewarded. Chairs need to be encouraged to offer their invaluable support through their creation of an environment conducive to effective teaching. Trained consultants, often though not invariably associated with a campus teaching center, should be recognized as the experts they are in instructional improvement and their activities facilitated. And new and junior faculty must be encouraged and helped with their teaching through programs recognizing their special needs and talents.

CONTENTS

FOREWORD

The title of this report, *Taking Teaching Seriously*, assumes that teaching is not taken seriously by a large number of higher education faculty and administrators. While many may feel uncomfortable with this contention, there are a number of conditions and assumptions that give evidence to support this position.

The first condition is the training of future college teachers and administrators. In both cases, courses or clinical experiences concerning the research and skills of teaching are seldom part of their formal education. While a few may have the experience of being a Teaching Assistant, the formal education and supervised training to become a TA is very limited. Compared with the practical training received in the basic skills of medicine or law, the training for teaching is almost non-existent. When faculty are asked how they learned to teach, the primary response is that they imitated the teaching style of a favorite professor. Role modeling is admirable, but it is hardly a substitute for a purposeful, supervised program to learn the theories and techniques of a specific professional skill.

A second condition is the visibility given to teaching. Under the guise of academic freedom, faculty establish a barrier of protection around their teaching activities. Rarely do faculty encourage peers, administrators, or teaching experts to visit their classroom, review their teaching performance, and suggest steps for improvement. Faculty and administrators often support the teaching privacy rights of the individual faculty member because they are not confident in their own ability to judge the teaching competency of their colleague. Instead, while the institutional leadership is talking about the importance of quality teaching, individual faculty members are being evaluated on their research agenda, the number of publications written, and the number of conference presentations given. These activities may not be valued over teaching, but because publications and conference presentations are more visible, easier to count, and usually have the legitimacy of peer review, they receive more emphasis because they are considered safe measurements of faculty performance.

The lack of emphasis given to making the skill of teaching an important consideration in judging faculty performance and a focus of continuous professional development is also rooted in three basic assumptions. First, when a faculty member is hired it is assumed the individual already possesses the necessary skills of teaching. This is especially true if that person holds a doctorate. A second assumption is that once a person has acquired the skills necessary to be a good teacher the individual always continues to be a good teacher. These two assumptions are rarely challenged because of the lack of an acceptable continuous means for institutions to measure quality teaching. The primary baseline standard of measurement is whether or not the students liked the teacher. Although research has supported the validity of student evaluation of teaching, these evaluations rarely assess the quality of teaching on a longitudinal basis or on the total content of a course in relation to the goals of the larger curriculum. Because of this lack of institutional standards and measurement of teaching, it is safer to assume that any deterioration in teaching performance is the responsibility of the individual professor and the institution has little responsibility for the continuous teaching development of its faculty.

This last assumption may be the most fallacious. It may really be true that when faculty are hired they do possess adequate teaching skills that last a lifetime. The question that is not asked is, "What type of students are they skilled to teach?" Faculty with graduate degrees receive their teaching skills at institutions that are often considerably different from where they begin their first faculty position. Add to this the consideration that, over the years, the type of student attending colleges and universities has changed considerably. The age, race, gender, education background, technological skills, and education expectations of today's students differ significantly from those of just ten years ago. Is it reasonable to expect that faculty trained at graduate institutions 20 years ago have the necessary teaching skills for the current student body?

Institutions should not make the assumption that the answer is yes to this question. Institutions need to be much more aggressive in their approach to ensuring the quality of teaching. In this report by Michael Paulsen, associate professor and coordinator of graduate programs in educational leadership at the University of New Orleans and Kenneth A. Feldman, professor of sociology at the State University of New York at Stony Brook, present a conceptual framework and process for instructional improvement which is carefully developed. This integrative study brings together the major research and literature on teaching and the means to make instructional improvement an integral part of an institution's culture.

Taking Teaching Seriously is not just a catchy title of a speech or book,it is the expectation that students, parents, employers and other stakeholders have for measuring the quality of an institution. With this monograph the authors detail the primary characteristics of a culture that is supportive of instructional improvement. Regrettably, few institutions have a majority of these characteristics. For those institutions that are serious about taking "teaching seriously", this report will be very useful in making these characteristics a permanent part of their culture.

Jonathan D. Fife
Series Editor,
Professor of Higher Education Administration and
Director, ERIC Clearinghouse on Higher Education

ACKNOWLEDGMENTS

We greatly appreciate the ongoing encouragement and support of Jonathan Fife, our series editor, before and during our work on this report. We are lucky, moreover, to have had a particularly good set of review panelists and consulting editors; their excellent comments and suggestions helped improve the report. And we are lucky to have families who are so supportive of our efforts; their comments and suggestions help improve our lives.

THE CHALLENGE OF INSTRUCTIONAL IMPROVEMENT

A movement that K. Patricia Cross labeled "Taking Teaching Seriously" is spreading throughout the country. Campus after campus is reexamining its commitment to teaching and beginning to explore ways that teaching might be rewarded and improved (Edgerton, Hutchings, and Quinlan 1991, p. 1).

During the 1980s, several influential national reports raised questions about the quality of undergraduate education (see, e.g., Association of American Colleges 1985; W.J. Bennett 1984; Boyer 1987; National Institute of Education 1984). Among the many challenges emerging from these reports were recommendations that higher education place a high priority on the quality of college teaching and its improvement. Most colleges and universities across the country are now striving to meet this challenge. The call for instructional improvement has come in many forms and from a variety of sources. In addition to the recommendations in the formal reports produced by government agencies, foundations, and professional associations, increasingly urgent pleas for improvement in the quality of college teaching have come from faculty, disciplinary societies, university task forces, campus administrators, students and their families, state legislatures, and governing boards. While all of these groups share a concern for greater quality in college teaching, they differ in terms of their reasons for being concerned.

Faculty have wrestled for more than a century with the conflict surrounding their roles as teachers and researchers.

The Concern about Quality

Expressions of concern about the quality of college teaching arise from the faculty themselves, especially because of their attitudes about the relative importance to be placed on teaching and research. Faculty have wrestled for more than a century with the conflict surrounding their roles as teachers and researchers (Austin and Gamson 1983; Hawkins 1979). In 1992–93, 77 percent of 29,771 faculty at 289 colleges and universities reported that their primary interests were "very heavily in" or "leaning toward" teaching, while only 24 percent expressed the same sort of primary interest in research (Dey, Ramirez, Korn, and Astin 1993, p. 10). Among faculty at public universities, 97.8 percent reported that "to be a good teacher" was a "very important" or "essential" professional goal (p. 35), but only 5.4 percent of these faculty reported that the statement "faculty are rewarded for being good teachers" was "very descriptive" of their college or university (pp. 38, 94). These findings are consistent with those of another survey of 5,450 professors at 306 colleges and universities, where 71 percent reported that their interests were "primarily in" or "leaning toward" teaching but only 29 percent reported the same level of interest in research (Carnegie Foundation 1989, p. 43). Furthermore, 35 percent of all faculty and over 50 percent of faculty at doctoral and research universities agreed with the statement, "The pressure to publish reduces the quality of teaching at my university" (p. 51). Clearly, faculty are themselves concerned about instruction and its improvement.

These preferences and concerns continue in the face of well-documented relationships between faculty income and the time spent on teaching relative to research. A recent study of 8,383 faculty from 424 colleges and universities reveals that the faculty who spend the least time on teaching and the most time on research receive the highest incomes, while the lowest-paid faculty are those who devote the most time to teaching and the least time to research (Fairweather 1993, pp. 3–8; see also Ratcliff and Associates 1995).

Scholars at the Carnegie Foundation recently developed an innovative reformulation of the concept of scholarship to include several dimensions. This multidimensional construct includes both a scholarship of research as well as a scholarship of teaching (Boyer 1990; Rice 1991). The report, *Scholarship Reconsidered,* has stimulated disciplinary societies and universities across the country to restructure faculty roles and responsibilities so that excellent teaching and improved instruction can be promoted, evaluated, and rewarded on a level comparable to research (Adam and Roberts 1993; R. Diamond 1994; Diamond and Adam 1995; Roberts, Wergin, and Adam 1993). Faculty support for such efforts appears to be strong. In the Carnegie Foundation survey mentioned earlier, for example, 69 percent of faculty at research universities and 77 percent of faculty at doctoral universities agreed with the statement, "At my institution, we need better ways, besides publications, to evaluate the scholarly performance of the faculty" (1989, p. 52).

Further support for instructional improvement comes from campus administrators, particularly central academic administrators. A relatively recent national survey that studied the perceptions of faculty, chairs, deans, and central academic administrators with regard to the relative importance of teaching and research found that, on average, faculty, chairs, and deans are very similar in their beliefs that teaching and research are of equal importance (Gray, Froh, and Diamond 1992). Although they perceive that their universities currently place much greater emphasis on research than on teaching, they believe their universities should move in the direction of equality or balance between emphases on teaching and research. In contrast, central academic administrators on average expressed a clear preference for greater emphasis on teaching than on research. Although they perceive that their universities currently place a somewhat greater emphasis on research than on teaching, they believe their universities should move in the direction of greater emphasis on teaching than on research (pp. 5–7). "It may well be that central administrators really value teaching. It also may be that these administrators have been influenced by the attitudes expressed in the national media and the various national reports, as well as by pressure from students and their parents, which call for a renewed emphasis on undergraduate teaching in America's research universities" (p. 7).

Students and their families express an understandable concern about the quality of undergraduate education—a product whose price, in the form of tuition, persistently increases at rates exceeding growth in the consumer price index (Halstead 1989; Hauptman 1990; Paulsen 1991). And this concern could have been heightened by provocative public literature like *ProfScam* (Sykes 1988).

State legislatures and governing boards hear the clamor of the public for improvement in instruction, yet they must contend with revenue shortfalls and the imposition of budget cutbacks (Halstead 1992; Hines 1988). Perhaps because of this situation, their reaction often takes the form of establishing procedures for obtaining evidence of improvements in both the quality and quantity of teaching. A growing number of states and institutions are now conducting formal studies of faculty workload and instructional productivity (Cage 1995; Winkler 1992), but it is important that all parties be aware that increases in the "quantity" of enrollments or graduates per unit of faculty input, through higher teaching loads and higher student-faculty ratios, could result in deceptive gains in instructional productivity (Johnstone

1993; St. John 1994). More students taught does not necessarily lead to superior student learning outcomes. Meaningful gains in instructional productivity can occur only when the "quality" of students' learning experiences (valued learning outcomes) increases per unit of faculty input. This gain in the quality of learning can, of course, occur through improved instructional effectiveness. Thus, genuine gains in instructional productivity can occur if the quality of learning improves as a result of better instruction while the quantity of students remains constant. Gains in productivity can also occur if increases in the quality of learning, again because of improved instruction, are sufficient to offset any detrimental effects of a larger number of students per class.

Teaching Culture and Strategies
For Improving Instruction

The phrase "taking teaching seriously" is from a celebrated address delivered by K. Patricia Cross at the 1986 AAHE National Conference on Higher Education in Washington, D.C. Some of the far-reaching ideas in her presentation emphasized not only the importance of efforts to increase the quality of college teaching, but also the need for what we would call—from the perspective of the mid-1990s—"a teaching culture" that supports and values such efforts.

> *The teacher-scholar was pushed off stage by the research scientist in the 1960s, and the results, whatever they may have done for advancement of knowledge, have not been salutary for undergraduate education. . . . One result of this turn is that dedicated teachers no longer feel valued by their institutions. For undergraduate education to improve, teachers will need the wholehearted support of their institutions, starting with a commitment to evaluate teaching performance in decisions to hire, promote, and tenure faculty members* (Cross 1986, p. 12).

Cross can be interpreted as also recommending the implementation of strategies that could both improve instruction and help create more supportive teaching cultures on college and university campuses. Based on the new epistemology of practice presented by Donald Schon in *The Reflective Practitioner* (1983), for example, she suggested that college teachers become classroom researchers. These college instructors would view their classrooms as laboratories where they could continually collect information about what and how their students learn in relation to what and how they are being taught. Through careful reflection, instructors could establish meaningful connections between their own teaching behaviors and their students' learning processes and outcomes. Such efforts would also illuminate the content-specific characteristics of effective teaching in a particular discipline. Because departmental colleagues would now have the results of ongoing instructional experiments to report, "faculty meetings might well become seminars for the improvement of teaching" (Cross 1986, p. 14). Classroom research is one of the many ways in which feedback on teaching and learning effectiveness can be obtained, and such feedback is a key ingredient of a wide range of strategies to improve instruction.

> *The involvement of teachers in searching for new knowledge about teaching effectiveness also begins to build a foundation for improved evaluation of teaching, an essential ingredient in rewarding teaching in promotion and tenure decisions. . . . I can think of no action that would do quite as much for the improvement of teaching and learning as to let a thousand classroom laboratories bloom across the nation. . . . That would be taking teaching seriously, and it would move us toward our goal of quality education for all* (Cross 1986, p. 14).

As scholars have come to understand these ideas better, in part through an expanding literature of experience and experiment, the underlying themes of teaching culture and instructional improvement strategies have taken on greater importance. In the intervening years, researchers and practitioners have begun to develop a more refined appreciation of the content of a teaching culture, and they have expanded the range and examined the effectiveness of many strategies to improve instruction. Such strategies are ways for faculty to traverse successfully the several steps of planned change in the effectiveness of teaching. And various aspects of teaching cultures can enhance or diminish faculty efforts to improve teaching at each phase of instructional improvement. For example, the campus teaching center has shown itself to be an important characteristic of supportive teaching cultures that promote the faculty's involvement in improving instruction (Austin 1990b). Moreover, just as faculty efforts to improve instruction are nurtured by supportive teaching cultures, such efforts in turn probably help strengthen the existing teaching cultures.

Purpose and Organization of This Report

To respond meaningfully to the call for instructional improvement, a revitalized agenda is in order. It is time to draw upon the extensive experience of instructional developers (Boice 1992b; Brinko 1993; Lewis and Povlacs 1988; Weimer 1990). What these developers have learned about the *process* of instructional improvement and the *strategies* that effectively energize that process should be made easily accessible to all faculty at all times. Moreover, to make nationwide instructional improvement possible, faculty and other academic leaders must work to change their campus teaching cultures so that teaching is no longer undervalued (Diamond and Adam 1993, 1995; Edgerton 1993; Hutchings 1993b; Rice and Austin 1990; Seldin 1990). A primary purpose of this report is to serve as a stimulator of renewed interest in instructional improvement and a source of guidance, direction, and ideas for deans, department chairs, and other faculty leaders who want to initiate, expand, or revitalize instructional improvement on their campuses.

Because a great deal has been written about college teaching and its improvement, this report is highly (and quite deliberately) selective in what it presents; it includes little research or thought that does not have fairly direct implications for teaching and how it might be improved. For example, the discussion of a "student voice" focuses considerable attention on the research on student ratings in their *formative* use in helping teachers to improve their instruction rather than on the reliability and validity of student ratings as *summative* measures (as reviewed in, for example, Feldman 1976, 1977, 1978, 1983, 1984; Marsh 1984, 1987; Marsh and Dunkin 1992) to be used, say, in personnel decisions.

Whenever possible, this report emphasizes the results and implications of research in an area of discussion. Within this empirical approach, the report stresses the results of various research integrations, meta-analyses, and other sorts of research reviews. Many single pieces of research have also been included—particularly those that have been especially important to the development of an area, relate most directly to a section's theme(s), present distinctive data or otherwise fill certain research gaps in the field, or have important implications for practice and are likely to be useful for teachers, chairs, and administrators. Certain selective ideas, propositions, speculations, and suggestions are also included that have not necessarily been verified by research but about which there is some degree of consensus among analysts and practitioners about their usefulness. At the same time, particularly fresh approaches that appear to have some potential to improve teaching are included. In brief, opinion is not avoided so long as it is *informed* opinion.

This report is intended to provide practical answers to the question of what deans, department chairs, and other faculty leaders can do to encourage and support efforts to improve instruction for individual instructors. It thus provides (1) an examination of the nature of instructional improvement and the challenge of motivating faculty to improve their teaching, make the necessary changes in their teaching, and maintain those changes; (2) an exploration of the important factors in the creation of a supportive campus teaching culture; (3) detailed explanations and illustrations of five sources of feedback for improving instruction (teachers themselves, students, colleagues, consultants, and chairs) based on a review of the literature on successful practices; and (4) an analysis of the special needs of new and junior faculty for instructional improvement.

THE PROCESS OF INSTRUCTIONAL IMPROVEMENT

Models of Change

Much of this section examines the nature of instructional improvement for individual teachers and the personal dynamics involved in the process. How is it that teachers become motivated to want to improve their teaching and to produce and maintain actual changes in behavior? Improving teaching is not solely the responsibility of individual faculty members and does not lie only in the realm of self-generating individual change. A variety of group, social-structural, and cultural forces are involved, yet ultimately it is the individual college teacher who must change something about his or her behavior if instruction is to be improved. This section explores the process of individual change that underlies instructional improvement.

Several useful models of instructional improvement have been developed. Each takes a different perspective and offers distinctive insights into the nature of the process. One approach has been to describe instructional improvement from a faculty perspective, explaining how college teachers interact with their environment in a familiar feedback loop (Menges 1991). Teachers receive input or feedback about their effectiveness from their environment, compare it with their internal standards for performance, and then restore equilibrium by changing their output (teaching behavior), feedback input, or internal performance standards.

> *Feedback loops are easily discerned in instructional settings. Imagine that examination scores create dissonance because the teacher (comparator) finds them below her standard. She may deal with the discrepancy by gathering additional kinds of data, ultimately concluding that students are not deficient after all. Thus, equilibrium is restored. She may reflect on what she expects of students, decide that these expectations are too high, and adjust her expectations to restore equilibrium. Finally, she may schedule review sessions . . . to raise students' performance, thereby restoring equilibrium. . . . Many college teachers do this naturally. They solicit information as feedback; they reflect on their expectations, beliefs, and values; and they experiment with different ways of teaching* (Menges 1991, p. 27).

Another model of instructional improvement postulates that formative evaluation (informative feedback) promotes optimum improvement in the effectiveness of teaching when four conditions are met (Centra 1993).

Through formative evaluation the teachers must first learn something new about their teaching performance (new knowledge). Second, they must value the information; this generally means they must have confidence in the source and in the evaluation process (value). Third, teachers must understand how to make the changes called for (how to change). And finally, teachers must be motivated to make the changes (motivation). . . . This does not mean that improvements will not occur if only two or three conditions are fulfilled; however, in those instances, the changes are not likely to be so dramatic. The model can best be understood as a linear progression of the four conditions, with a final return loop. . . . The loop signifies that motivation not only affects the improvements but also may cause teachers to seek additional new knowledge about their instructional effectiveness (Centra 1993, pp. 9, 14–15).

A third model takes the straightforward approach of describing five steps that teachers must go through to improve their instructional effectiveness (Weimer 1990). While the previous two models were primarily explanatory or theoretical, this model is clearly more descriptive.

First, faculty members develop instructional awareness, a clear understanding of the instructional strategies, techniques, and practices they use and the assumptions about teaching and learning implicit in them. Second, they gather information from students and peers to accomplish three objectives. The input from others (a) clarifies and elaborates further the instructor's own understanding of his or her teaching; (b) . . . offers feedback as to the impact of the policy, practice, behavior, or activity on the person offering the input; and (c) . . . generates a pool of alternative ideas—other(and perhaps more effective) ways to accomplish the instructor's objectives. Third, faculty members make choices about changes. This involves identifying the teaching strategies, techniques, or practices to be changed and the instructional alternatives that are appropriate solutions for the particular teacher to try. Fourth, the faculty member implements the changes systematically and incrementally. Fifth, the faculty member assesses the impact of the alterations (Weimer 1990, p. 34).

These models, providing us with meaningful ways of organizing our thoughts about instructional improvement, can be seen as implicitly grounded in the general theory of change in human systems pioneered by Lewin (1947) and elaborated and refined by Schein in studies of management development (1961), general personal change (1964), improvement in professional education (1972), organizational change (1992), and human relations training (Schein and Bennis 1965). This general theory of change comprises the three stages of unfreezing, changing, and refreezing.

Unfreezing: Motivating Change
During the unfreezing stage, the motivation to change is created when three criteria have been met. First, an individual experiences "disconfirmation" cues from his or her environment, that is, information indicating that the individual's present attitudes and behaviors are not achieving the goals or producing the results that would be consistent with his or her current self-image. The assumptions and beliefs a person holds about himself or herself (the self-image), however, are related to the assumptions and beliefs the person holds about the nature of a particular situation and others who are relevant to that situation. Therefore, the unfreezing process can be initiated through disconfirmation cues related to any of the aspects of a total situation (Schein 1964, p. 364). Second, the individual "compares" information on the outcomes of his or her actual behavior to outcomes that the individual desires and considers important or ideal. When this incongruence leads to a sense of guilt, anxiety, or inadequacy related to not achieving some aspect of one's ideal self-image, it suggests that the disconfirming cues have had an impact on some of the individual's primary sources of motivation. A desire to reduce or eliminate such disequilibrium could lead to a motivation to change. In order to be so motivated, a third condition must also be met: The individual must feel a sense of psychological "safety" associated

The individual "compares" information on the outcomes of his or her actual behavior to outcomes that the individual desires and considers important or ideal.

with attempts to change. The person must be able to envision ways to change that will produce results that reestablish his or her positive self-image without feeling any loss of integrity or identity. "One essential component of this feeling of safety is that we finally see a way to work on the problem or see a direction of learning that we had not seen before" (Schein 1992, p. 301).

Unfreezing could motivate a professor to improve his or her teaching if disconfirming cues relate to important goals in a way that affects motivational patterns related to the professor's need to see himself or herself as an effective teacher. Evidence consistently indicates that college professors, like many other professionals, are motivated or satisfied in their jobs primarily as a result of the intrinsic rewards of academic work (Austin and Gamson 1983; B. Clark 1987a; McKeachie 1979, 1982; Olsen 1993). Intrinsic "motivation is based on the innate need to be competent and self-determining. . . . This basic need leads people to situations and activities that interest them, that provide optimal challenges, that allow them to learn and achieve" (Deci and Ryan 1982, p. 28).

The intrinsically rewarding nature of faculty work, including teaching, can be clearly seen in terms of the "job characteristics model" of intrinsic motivation theory (Hackman and Oldham 1976). An individual, such as a college professor, who experiences a high need for personal growth and development will be more intrinsically motivated "to the extent that he *learns* (knowledge of results) that he *personally* (experienced responsibility) has performed well on a task that he *cares about* (experienced meaningfulness)" (pp. 255–56). Knowledge of results is enhanced by the availability of informative feedback on performance. A person's sense of personal responsibility for outcomes depends on the extent to which he or she experiences autonomy or self-determination in performing the various elements of the task. Finally, the perceived meaningfulness of work depends on the presence of three characteristics of the job: skill variety, task identity, and task significance. Skill variety is the "degree to which a job requires a variety of different activities...[that] involve the use of a number of different skills and talents." Task identity is "the degree to which the job requires completion of a 'whole' and identifiable piece of work; that is, doing a job from beginning to end with a visible outcome." And task significance is the "degree to which the job has a substantial impact on the lives or work of other people, whether in the immediate organization or in the external environment" (p. 257).

It is common, for example, for an instructor's first concern with disconfirming cues to arise from end-of-semester student ratings of their teaching. When the instructor compares these ratings with his or her own assumptions and beliefs about his or her teaching effectiveness, the instructor may find them to fall below his or her internal standards. Such disconfirming cues could easily affect the instructor's intrinsic motivational needs related to perceptions of competence, self-determination, and the meaningfulness or significance of his or her work. As a result, the instructor might feel discomfort or a sense of inadequacy and desire to explore change as a way of restoring equilibrium. The instructor must also see a way to experiment without impairing his or her self-image. Suppose a close colleague had shared with the instructor information about his own similar situation a year earlier; suppose further that the instructor had observed him change some factors and get higher ratings in the current year. Now the instructor can see a safe path to change that might well produce results that would reduce or eliminate his or her current discomfort.

A key factor in leading this instructor toward motivation to change is the presence of opportunities for interaction and discussion among colleagues about their teaching experiences. Opportunities for interaction with peers regarding teaching have been shown to be an important characteristic of a supportive teaching culture (LaCelle-Peterson and Finkelstein 1993; Massy, Wilger, and Colbeck 1994). Clearly, then, the content of a teaching culture can have an important impact, even on this first stage of the overall instructional improvement process.

Changing: Making It Happen
After the unfreezing stage has produced a "motivation to change, the person . . . will search out new ideas and new information . . . to develop new attitudes and responses [behaviors] that will be rewarded or confirmed" (Schein 1972, p. 79). During the changing stage, an individual learns new attitudes and behaviors through the acquisition and interpretation of this new information. The individual col-

lects informative feedback from one or more sources to cognitively redefine the situation or revise the assumptions and beliefs held about oneself, others, and the relevant situation. As a result, some cognitive redefinition precedes each experiment with new behavior the person makes. Cognitive redefinition and resulting behavioral change result from two primary mechanisms: scanning and identification (Schein 1964, 1972, 1992; Schein and Bennis 1965). The mechanism of *scanning* involves collecting informative feedback from more than one (perhaps a variety) of the types of sources or persons in the environment. From each type of source, an individual collects the feedback that best fits the needs of the individual relevant to a particular situation he or she faces. In contrast, the mechanism of *identification* is based on the collection of informative feedback from only one source (or type of source) with whom the individual has come to identify. Information from this source alone—perhaps a role model—shapes cognitive redefinition. These mechanisms characterize the processes by which individuals attempt to locate solutions to the disequilibrium initiated during the unfreezing stage.

For example, to obtain additional informative feedback to guide his or her experiments at change, the instructor in our example could begin the next term by collecting informal feedback from his or her students early in the semester (Clark and Bekey 1979). Next, the instructor could reflect on this feedback (Chism and Sanders 1986) and then ask a trusted colleague to sit in on his or her class to obtain additional feedback from a peer (Katz and Henry 1988). Third, the instructor could visit with a teaching consultant at the campus teaching center to acquire additional guidance on how to change his or her teaching using the multiple sources of feedback the instructor has collected by scanning the environment (Lewis and Povlacs 1988). Finally, a supportive department chair could invite this instructor to sit in on one of the chair's own classes, share his or her own ideas about instructional improvement, and help the instructor develop additional plans for change (Vavrus, Grady, and Creswell 1988). In this example, the instructor assessed his or her instructional experiments by scanning the environment for informative feedback from five different sources: self, students, colleagues, consultants, and the department chair.

A central feature of this instructor's actual experimentation with change is the availability and use of multiple sources of informative feedback and guidance. When departmental and institutional teaching cultures are rich with opportunities to assess teaching, instructors can more easily experiment with their teaching and successfully scan the environment for various sources of informative feedback. Serious and rigorous evaluative information from different sources, such as students and peers, is an important characteristic of a supportive teaching culture (Massy, Wilger, and Colbeck 1994). Departments and campuses rich with information assessing teaching create an important aspect of a supportive teaching culture—sometimes referred to as the "culture of assessment" (Braskamp and Ory 1994). "In a culture of assessment, faculty members profit from discussion and reflection about how their individual achievements contribute to their personal gain and the common good" (p. 23).

Refreezing: Sustaining Change

After cognitive redefinition and experiments with new behavior have been carried out, further informative feedback is collected as part of the final stage of overall change. The refreezing stage refers to the ways in which additional informative feedback on new behaviors either encourages or discourages the maintenance of these changes. New behaviors can be sustained through two basic mechanisms: integration and reconfirmation. "Whatever new response [behavior] is attempted, it must fit into the total personality of the individual attempting it [integration], and it must fit sufficiently into the culture of which that person is a member to be confirmed and reinforced by others [reconfirmation]" (Schein 1972, p. 81).

For instance, suppose the instructor in our example does receive significantly higher ratings from students at the end of the next semester, particularly in the areas of teaching that he or she had specifically targeted for improvement. If the instructor once again perceives himself or herself to be competent and self-determining and feels that his or her teaching is meaningful and significant work, then the changes are likely to be integrated into the instructor's total personality, thereby helping to sustain the changed behavior. As the theory of change indicates, however, the teaching culture might have to supply reconfirming data for the instructor's instructional improvements to be sustained indefinitely. The instructor's efforts to improve, as well as his or her new teaching behaviors, might need to be supported by others in the environment.

The teaching culture provides informative feedback in various ways that reconfirm equilibrium and encourage the maintenance of change. For example, the dean or department chair might ask this instructor and several of the instructor's colleagues to lead a panel discussion of their experiences with instructional improvement at the next college or departmental faculty meeting. Opportunities to discuss teaching experiences with peers strengthens an instructor's intrinsic rewards from teaching, thereby contributing to a more supportive teaching culture (Froh, Menges, and Walker 1993). The panel discussion would also help communicate to these and other faculty that the administration is committed to improving instruction within the college or department. Administrative commitment has been found to be directly related to the success of efforts to improve instruction (Eble and McKeachie 1985). Further, the efforts to improve these instructors' teaching may be given serious consideration in evaluating the faculty. A strong connection between the evaluation of teaching effectiveness and promotion and tenure decisions is a characteristic of a supportive teaching culture (Jenrette and Napoli 1994; Wolverton and Richardson 1992).

A Model of Instructional Improvement that Includes Individual, Interpersonal, and Group Forces

Figure 1 illustrates a "general change model" that includes the recognition of a teaching culture within which sources of informative feedback—self, students, colleagues, consultants, and chairs—influence the various stages of the process of change. In several ways the model provides an underlying analytic framework for examining instructional improvement. First, for many years parts of this model have proven to be useful and popular for explaining human change across a wide variety of settings. Second, the model explicitly acknowledges the important influence of the content of organizational culture on the initiation, implementation, and persistence of behavioral change in human systems. This attribute makes the model especially useful as a heuristic

FIGURE 1

THE PROCESS OF INSTRUCTIONAL IMPROVEMENT

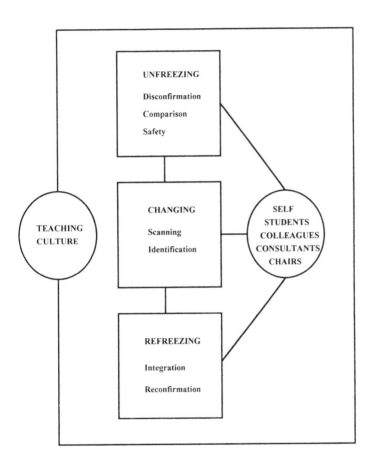

device for exploring the influence of particular aspects of the teaching culture, such as the formal use of teaching portfolios in faculty evaluation, on the process of change (Hutchings 1993a; Seldin 1993). Third, because of its comprehensiveness and generalizability, the model encompasses many or all of the concepts and component parts of other models implicitly or explicitly derived from it. As a result, it is flexible enough to examine the importance of informative feedback at all stages of the process of change, which means that all of the primary sources of informative feedback (self, students, colleagues, consultants, and chairs) can be conceived of as having a potential bearing at every stage of the process. This feature is especially important, because most strategies for improving instruction can be discussed and even categorized according to their particular sources or means of acquiring informative feedback and guidance for change (Braskamp, Brandenburg, and Ory 1984; Centra 1993). Fourth, it explicitly considers the important influence of individual differences (for example, different professional goals during different stages of development) on the process of change, allowing the model to be applied to the special needs of particular subgroups of faculty, such as new and junior faculty (Sorcinelli and Austin 1992).

*In spring . . . 1990, the American Association for
Higher Education (AAHE) established a new program
aimed at improving college teaching and learning.
Though now encompassing a variety of projects and
lines of work, the Teaching Initiative (as we call it)
continues to pursue a single, unifying vision: what is
needed for improvement of instruction is a culture in
which teaching and learning are the subject of serious,
sustained discussion and debate; where people talk
about teaching, inquire into its effects, and work
together for improvement* (Hutchings 1993b, p. 63).

*I like the way the chair of the English Department at
Stanford put it: "What we're trying to do," he said, "is to
create a culture of teaching, one in which the conversations, the priorities [and, I would add, the rituals and
kinship systems] of the department have teaching at their
center." . . . To change academic culture in this way will
not be easy. But colleges and universities have always
taken justifiable pride in their commitment to inquiry
and criticism in all fields, even those where dogma and
habit make real scrutiny uncomfortable. Now we must
turn this tough scrutiny on our own practices, traditions,
and culture. Only by doing so will we make teaching
truly central to higher education* (Shulman 1993, p. 7).

Concepts of Organizational Culture

College instructors do not teach in a vacuum. They are part
of an organization whose culture could both positively and
negatively affect their teaching. The intellectual origins of
modern cultural analysis of organizations are predominantly
in anthropology and sociology (Allaire and Firsirotu 1984;
Ouchi and Wilkins 1985). Anthropologists and other ethnographic scholars have long studied cultures, but it was not
until the early 1980s that a growing number of organizational
researchers began to view organizations as "culture-bearing
milieux" (Louis 1992, p. 509). The cultural perspective in the
study of organizations challenges and contradicts the
assumptions and approaches to research associated with the
traditional, rational-structural perspectives on organizational
behavior (Sergiovanni 1992; Shafritz and Ott 1992). One
important and distinctive contribution of the cultural perspective is that it draws our attention to the "expressive, nonra-

tional . . . subjective, interpretive aspects of organizational life" (Smircich 1983, p. 355).

Although "the essence of a group's culture is its pattern of shared, taken-for-granted basic assumptions, the culture will manifest itself at the levels of observable artifacts and shared espoused values, norms, and rules of behavior" (Schein 1992, p. 26). Thus, the content of organizational culture can be analyzed at various levels along a continuum extending from the most implicit essence of culture to the most explicit expressions of that culture. The deepest level of cultural content is the essence or "substance" of organizational culture—the webs of shared meanings that constitute deeply embedded assumptions and beliefs common to members of a group. While the substance of an organization's culture is largely implicit, intangible, and unconscious, it is expressed to group members on a more tangible surface level in terms of more explicit cultural "forms"—artifacts, such as rites and ceremonials, and other symbols that are more readily observable (Trice and Beyer 1984, p. 654). The substance of culture comprises the tacit underlying assumptions, beliefs, values, philosophies, and ideologies that essentially shape organizational behavior. The forms of culture include a variety of observable artifacts, such as rites, rituals, ceremonials, myths, sagas, stories, language, gestures, architecture, informal and formal rules, practices, norms, patterns of behavior and interaction, and other symbolic processes (Kuh and Whitt 1988; Peterson, Cameron, Jones, Mets, and Ettington 1986; Peterson and Spencer 1990; Shafritz and Ott 1992; Tierney and Rhoads 1993; Trice and Beyer 1984). Cultural forms provide most of the available evidence about the core or substance of culture.

Although culture can and should be thought of as a source of stability in organizations in many ways (Hatch 1993; Parsons and Platt 1973; Schein 1992), it is important to remember that organizational cultures are constantly evolving, being constructed and reconstructed, both shaping human interaction as well as being shaped by it (Jelinek, Smircich, and Hirsch 1983, p. 331). And many approaches have been recommended and applied in the promotion of change in organizational cultures (Chaffee and Tierney 1988; Deal and Kennedy 1982; Hatch 1993; Kilmann, Saxton, Serpa, and Associates 1985; Peterson et al. 1986; Rhoads and Tierney 1992; Sathe 1983; Schein 1992; Trice and Beyer 1984).

As revealed in a "cultural audit," the shared basic assumptions constituting the essence, core, or substance of culture are very difficult to discern. Group members are not fully and consciously aware of basic cultural assumptions and therefore take them for granted, rarely challenging them or even thinking or talking about them. When asked about such assumptions, individuals have difficulty discussing them directly. Instead, they speak of their organization's distinctiveness by describing concrete examples of surface-level artifacts or expressions of deeper cultural content. Describing a familiar ritual or telling a story is their way of communicating what the culture means to them (Wilkins 1983).

Challenges in studying organizational culture thus arise "because culture is implicit, and we are all embedded in our own cultures. In order to observe organizational culture, the researcher must find its visible and explicit manifestations" (Masland 1985, p. 160). Such overt, tangible, and accessible cultural forms provide "windows on organizational culture" (p. 160). As a result, most researchers of organizational culture work hard to discern the meanings of the elusive, essential substance of culture through analysis of the cultural content that is expressed in more accessible, surface-level cultural forms. When studying the work culture of an organization, inquiries regarding the nature of work that is expected and the type of work that is rewarded can be particularly revealing (Wilkins 1983, p. 30).

The recent rediscovery of the cultural perspective for organizational analysis began in the late 1980s with some well-known applications to the study of business organizations (Deal and Kennedy 1982; Ouchi 1981; Peters and Waterman 1982). The findings of these studies supported the contention that strong, congruent cultures promote effective organizational performance. Following some early and well-known studies of the organizational cultures of academic institutions (B. Clark 1970, 1972; Riesman and Jencks 1962), a growing number of such studies began to appear in the late 1980s (Bergquist 1992; Cameron and Ettington 1988; Chaffee and Tierney 1988; Peterson and Spencer 1993; Rice and Austin 1988; Tierney 1988a). The study of subcultures within academic institutions began with the exploration of student cultures (Bushnell 1962; Clark and Trow 1966; Feldman 1972; Feldman and Newcomb 1969; Hughes,

Becker, and Geer 1962) and has expanded to include insights into various dimensions of faculty cultures (Austin 1990a; Boice 1992b; B. Clark 1985, 1987a, 1987b; Schuster and Bowen 1985; Tierney and Rhoads 1993; Wergin 1994; Whitt 1991) and, finally, cultural perspectives on the college presidency (Bensimon 1989; Tierney 1988b).

The Teaching Culture and Its Place
In Colleges and Universities

Many . . . well-researched and persuasive critiques of higher education focus on the inadequacy of our commitment to the quality of instruction and the limited prestige of teaching in the values and reward system of academic culture. . . . There are historic reasons for the gradual shift toward a research model on American campuses, particularly at institutions with graduate programs. But there is also compelling evidence that concern for teaching has never been absent or silent, even on these campuses. Instead, teaching has perhaps been submerged—and deserves to take its rightful place once again in our institutional culture (Shelton and DeZure 1993, p. 27).

From 1636 through the late 19th century, American colleges were predominantly teaching institutions, based largely on an adapted English model of higher education devoted to the development of the student as a whole person (Brubacher and Rudy 1968; Carnegie Commission 1973; Rudolph 1990). Essentially, a culture of student development (primitive by modern standards and concepts of college student development) was the dominant culture of American higher education for over two centuries. During this time, the teaching culture represented an important subculture of the overall collegiate culture, in some ways contributing to students' development and in other ways constraining it (Cowley 1958; Fuhrmann and Grasha 1983).

Two important developments in the late 19th and early 20th centuries promoted a reconstruction of the faculty work cultures in American institutions of higher education. First, thousands of new professors, who had been educated in Germany, joined our faculty ranks. These professors were greatly influenced by some powerful assumptions embedded in the cultures of German universities, and when these cultural influences were selectively combined, taken out of context, and adapted to the American university, research and the advancement of knowledge for its own sake became impressive and valued undertakings. The "practice of research became elevated into an all-encompassing ideal" (Veysey 1965, p. 127). Second, during the same period, faculty and administrators were shaping a distinctively American service ideal as an important mission of academic work. Reaching its zenith in the Progressive Era, this ideal placed research in the highly valued role of helping to solve society's problems. In effect, "the American university united two divergent conceptions of research" (Metzger 1961, p. 107).

From the perspective of cultural dynamics, the research ideal initially entered American institutions at the level of artifacts—faculty practices or behaviors—that met with success, as viewed by some members of the academy. When the appreciation of the value of such work spread among a wider audience, both inside and outside the university, a critical mass of group members began to espouse the value of research work. And when the ongoing success of these valued research activities began to be taken for granted, the high status of research became part of an underlying assumption about the kind of faculty work expected and rewarded (Hatch 1993; Schein 1992).

Based on his study of faculty culture in American higher education, the author of *The Academic Life: Small Worlds, Different Worlds* observes that the research ideal has resulted in "hierarchies of status" stretching from the highest-status research universities to other doctoral universities to comprehensive universities to liberal arts colleges to the lowest-status community colleges (B. Clark 1987a, p. xxvii). He further concludes that the "greatest paradox of academic work in modern America is that most professors teach most of the time, and large proportions of them teach all the time, but teaching is not the activity most rewarded by the academic profession nor most valued by the system at large" (pp. 98–99).

Institutions at all levels in the hierarchy express a desire for more of the prestige associated with the research ideal. This "research surge" has intensified in the past decade or two (Schuster and Bowen 1985, p. 16). Because of the large supply of new Ph.D.'s from top research universities who are already socialized into the research ideal, the desire on campus for research-related status is growing. But "the goal of becoming 'a leading research university' [has been] espoused explicitly at many doctoral-granting universities that are still some distance from achieving distinction" (Schuster and Bowen 1985, p. 16).

To some extent, pursuit of the prestige of the research ideal is even felt at institutions where the primary criterion for tenure and promotion has long been effective teaching. Faculty dedicated to the teaching imperatives of community colleges seek ways to keep up with advances in their disciplines, to be viewed as scholars, and to conduct some research (Palmer and Vaughan 1992; Vaughan and Palmer 1991). At the same time, research and other doctoral universities often refuse tenure to outstanding teachers because their research record is considered inadequate.

> *Such repetitive professional behavior on the part of the evaluating academics results not from personal willfulness but from the underlying structure of commitments and related rewards. . . . This underlying problem has not and will not go away. In the inability to reward undergraduate teaching, we find the Achilles heel of the American research university. . . . Serious reform that seeks . . . changes are somewhere on the drawing board in virtually every major university, challenging administrators and faculty to creatively alter rewards for the professoriate, even at the risk of creating a division between a teaching faculty and a research faculty. Some small gains are made in stiffening the teaching criterion in promotion decisions. But with competition for scholarly status powerfully concentrating the institutional mind, the tides run strong in the opposite direction* (B. Clark 1987a, pp. 265–66).

To the extent that the research-based hierarchies of status clearly affect the dominant culture of a higher education institution, the teaching culture of that college or university can be meaningfully viewed as a *sub*culture. Nearly every type of organization, including colleges and universities, is characterized by a dominant culture as well as one or more subcultures (Bergquist 1992; Gregory 1983; Sackmann 1992). The embedded values of an organization's dominant culture are manifested in observable artifacts that express the basic beliefs shared by most members. The subcultures that normally develop either support, contradict, or are largely independent of the shared values of the dominant culture of the organization.

Three types of subcultures have been identified: enhancing, countercultural, and orthogonal (Martin and Siehl 1983). An enhancing subculture can be found among organizational subgroups where members' commitment to the basic beliefs of the dominant culture is stronger than the commitment of other members of the organization (pp. 53–54). A supportive teaching culture is most likely to be an enhancing subculture in a community college or a small private college where the research ideal is weak and the teaching ideal is strong. In these highly teaching-oriented institutions, subgroups of faculty often actively support or serve on faculty or staff development committees and participate regularly and enthusiastically in a wide range of instructional improvement activities promoted by the committee and its administrative supporters.

A counterculture exists when some of the basic beliefs of a subgroup in the organization "present a direct challenge to the core values of a dominant culture. Thus a dominant culture and a counterculture exist in an uneasy symbiosis, taking opposite positions on value issues that are critically important to each of them" (Martin and Siehl 1983, p. 54). In larger doctoral and research universities, where the research-based, status-seeking ideal is prominent, a subculture highly supportive of teaching is more likely to match the characteristics of a counterculture. Faculty's perceptions of the conflicting work demands placed on them by the dominant research cultures and the teaching subcultures at such universities have been well documented (Bowen and Schuster 1986; Boyer 1990; Carnegie Foundation 1989; Dey et al. 1993; Gray, Froh, and Diamond 1992; Ratcliff and Associates 1995; Schuster and Bowen 1985).

Finally, "in an orthogonal subculture, the members would simultaneously accept the core values of the dominant culture and a separate, unconflicting set of values particular to themselves" (Martin and Siehl 1983, p. 54).

A president at a doctorate university, in commenting on the mission of his institutions, put it this way: "This

The embedded values of an organization's dominant culture are manifested in observable artifacts that express the basic beliefs shared by most members.

campus should be a place where both great teachers and great researchers function side by side. We should have the confidence to say, 'Look, you're a great researcher and we are eager to have you here doing what you do best.'" He then added, "We should also be able to say to a colleague, 'You are terrific with students, but you are not publishing. Still, we want you to help us perform an important mission on the campus.'" This is precisely the kind of division of labor that should be clarified and strengthened at doctorate-granting institutions (Boyer 1990, pp. 58–59).

In such a doctorate-granting university, which has traditionally adhered strongly to the research model, a supportive teaching culture would fit well the characteristics of an orthogonal subculture. In an orthogonal teaching subculture, for example, members of the relevant subgroup would be committed to both the basic beliefs of the dominant culture of research and to a set of shared beliefs regarding the importance of the contribution of teaching and instructional improvement to that culture.

The Teaching Culture: A Subculture or A Dominant Culture?

Research cultures are not the dominant culture at all colleges and universities, despite certain trends in that direction. In fact, the degree to which one or another culture is dominant in a school still varies across institutions of higher education. At some schools, a teaching culture could be *as* dominant as—or even *more* dominant than—the research culture. In addition, some recently published reports (see, in particular, Boyer 1990 and Pister 1991) have prompted many universities to begin the process of formulating new institutional policies that seek to restructure faculty roles and rewards so that quality of teaching and instructional improvement are promoted, evaluated, and rewarded on a level comparable to research (Roberts, Wergin, and Adam 1993). Regardless of which culture dominates at a particular school, it can still support (enhance), contradict (counter), or be neutral to (orthogonal) the other.

Some analysts maintain that teaching and research are mutually supportive (see, e.g., Leary 1959), whereas others take the opposite view that the two are mutually antagonistic (see, e.g., Cutten 1958). Perhaps neither is the case. A meta-analysis of a number of studies found that, when results were averaged across a number of different colleges and universities, the research productivity of individual faculty members was positively associated with their teaching effectiveness (as measured by the perceptions and evaluations of their students) but only to a very small degree ($r = +.12$) (Feldman 1987). On the basis of this small positive correlation between research productivity and teaching effectiveness, it could be maintained that the two are at best slightly beneficial to one another. But it could just as well be argued that the correlation is so small that for all practical purposes the variables in question are generally independent of each other.

Faculty obviously could separate themselves into more than just two cultures. Just as those interested in academia have come to realize that there are different types of scholarship—for example, research, teaching, application, and integration (see Boyer 1990; Rice 1991; Richlin 1993; Schon 1995)—so the possibility of a type of subculture or culture associated with each arises. One reconceptualization of scholarship uses the Parsonian four-function paradigm as an analytic framework from which to deduce a somewhat different set of categories of scholarship: research and graduate training; teaching; service; and academic citizenship (Paulsen and Feldman 1995). Again, each could well be associated with a separate culture on campus.

In recent years, institutions have been increasingly encouraged to capitalize on the diverse dimensions of scholarship. Some institutions might wish to focus their mission and their faculty's scholarship relatively more on one of these several dimensions than on others. Liberal arts colleges, comprehensive colleges, and research universities—as three different types of institutions—might wish to emphasize more the scholarly activities of teaching, service, and research, respectively. In contrast, some institutions might wish to encourage their individual faculty members to specialize in their most preferred scholarly activities—those that capitalize on their distinctive talents. This latter approach is appropriate for many doctoral universities to consider.

These institutions typically see themselves as being "in transition," embracing to a very large degree the

*research model. . . . [But] doctorate-granting institutions
need also to recognize professors who make exceptional
contributions to other scholarly areas: integration,
application, and teaching. At these institutions, perhaps
more than any others, the mosaic of talent should be
carefully considered* (Boyer 1990, p. 58).

Regardless of whether the teaching culture is the dominant
culture or a subordinate subculture at a particular school, and
regardless of whether it enhances, contradicts, or is orthogonal to other cultures or subcultures at the particular school,
the characteristics of a supportive teaching culture are of great
importance. The effectiveness of all strategies to improve
instruction clearly benefits from the presence of a culture that
supports teaching. The next subsection draws upon the wisdom, experience, and research generated by instructional
developers, administrators, faculty leaders, and other higher
education scholars to synthesize what has been learned about
the characteristics of a supportive teaching culture.

In Search of a Supportive Teaching Culture
Most research on the characteristics of cultures that support
teaching in today's colleges and universities has focused on
identifying forms or artifacts common to institutional or
departmental cultures that place a high value on teaching
and its improvement. In particular, the focus is primarily on
organizational structures, behaviors, interactions, documents,
policies, and practices that appear to be outward manifestations of the values, beliefs, and assumptions constituting
those academic cultures that promote, support, and reward
efforts to improve the quality of teaching. The research literature consists primarily of qualitative studies, case studies,
and surveys. In combination, these studies have consistently
identified a number of prominent characteristics of cultures
that support teaching and its improvement. Eight of them
are especially salient.

Commitment and support from high-level administrators
To promote the improvement of instruction, the unambiguous commitment and support of senior administrators is necessary. It is important that "teaching improvement activities
[be] given high visibility by the senior administration in order

to illustrate their importance" (Wright and O'Neil 1994, p. 26). High-level administrators perform the critical role of communicating the institution's mission in terms of the value placed on teaching. In general, faculty need to be convinced that the administration's positive rhetoric about excellent teaching "is not merely polite language to satisfy various external constituents and that it will indeed drive the reward system" (Armour 1995, p. 20). An evaluative study of the Lilly Endowment Teaching Fellows Program at 30 research universities illustrates the important impact that supportive senior administrators can have on the way teaching is valued.

> *One example is provided by the University of Massachusetts, where, even in the midst of serious financial constraints, the teaching fellows program has continued without external funding and, additionally, a center for teaching has been established. This success owes much to the considerable involvement of the associate vice chancellor for academic affairs in the program, especially during its earliest years, and his strong public advocacy of the importance of teaching at the institution and the contribution made by the teaching fellows program* (Austin 1992, p. 83).

A recent case study of the efforts of the University of Massachusetts at Amherst to "encourage a culture on campus that values teaching" has also emphasized how important it is for the campus community—especially faculty—to feel that the administration clearly values teaching highly (Aitken and Sorcinelli 1994, p. 64). The findings also indicate, however, that at research universities such as this one, administrators might be hesitant to speak out in favor of the value of teaching because they are concerned that faculty could perceive that the administration does not adequately support the institution's research mission. Clearly, faculty and administrative support for teaching and its improvement are interdependent. In other words, faculty and administrators must come together to establish shared values about teaching.

Faculty involvement, shared values, and a sense of ownership

While the strong support of senior administrators is an essential component of a culture that encourages the improvement of instruction, the widespread involvement of faculty in every aspect of planning and implementing improved teaching is necessary to increase the chances for shared values between administrators and faculty. In-depth case studies of 10 liberal arts colleges where faculty were highly committed to teaching revealed that "participatory leadership" and "organizational structures" that encouraged "active involvement of faculty in making important institutional decisions" were common characteristics of the teaching cultures of these exemplary colleges (Rice and Austin 1990, pp. 28–29).

Miami-Dade Community College's Teaching and Learning Project was the first recipient of TIAA-CREF's Theodore M. Hesburgh Award for the most outstanding faculty development program dedicated to the enhancement of the quality of teaching. The "blueprint for change" underlying this project serves as a model for all colleges and universities seeking to create a culture supportive of teaching. The project director and a member of the steering committee describe how they worked to promote shared values about the importance of teaching among members of the campus community:

> *The first area to be addressed was that of institutional values related to teaching and learning. . . . The Teaching/Learning Values Subcommittee . . . began with an intensive research review of college-produced documents, self-studies, and material written about Miami-Dade. From this review they identified implicit values [that] were then placed into a survey and sent to all college personnel as well as a sampling of students and community members. Several cycles of activity followed . . . [and] a set of seven institutional values related to teaching/learning . . . articulated. . . . This values document then became the cornerstone of the entire project* (Jenrette and Napoli 1994, p. 6).

The results of case studies at 12 other community colleges indicate that institutional cultures characterized by shared values between administrators and faculty "centered on the importance of promoting [students'] achievement" are the most likely to manifest faculty behaviors that promote students' learning (Richardson 1993, p. 106). Further, among colleges and universities participating in the Bush Foundation Faculty Development Project, researchers found that institutional cultures characterized by shared faculty-administrative leadership that promoted a sense of "faculty ownership" had more successful faculty development programs (Eble and McKeachie 1985, p. 216).

A broader definition of scholarship

After nearly a full century since the construct of scholarship was given its contemporary meaning, the 1990s have witnessed growing efforts to reconceptualize and expand the meaning of scholarship (Boyer 1990; Lynton and Elman 1987; Paulsen and Feldman 1995; Rice 1991; Schon 1995). The results of four recent case studies of institutions ranging from a large research university to a small liberal arts college indicate that one of the factors that influences the relationship between the culture of a campus and the value it places on teaching is "an appropriate balance between teaching and scholarship" (Armour 1995, p. 20). For example, at Syracuse University in 1992, Chancellor Kenneth A. Shaw promoted a broader conception of scholarship that was to include discovery, integration, application, and teaching. In response, academic departments have been reformulating their evaluation of faculty to take into account a broader range of scholarly activities. In particular, research on effective teaching in one's own discipline is now given more attention during evaluation. A study of 10 exemplary liberal arts colleges found that each college in its own way challenged the restrictive view that scholarship equals research. These schools value as scholarship various forms of faculty work, including teaching, research, and service. This expanded view "allows faculty to build on their own scholarly strengths and be rewarded for them" (Rice and Austin 1990, p. 33).

A teaching demonstration or pedagogical colloquium as part of the hiring process

Campus cultures that highly value teaching regularly include some demonstration of effective teaching as part of interviewing and hiring new faculty (Jenrette and Napoli 1994; Rice and Austin 1988). A recent survey of faculty development professionals found that the policy of "hiring practices [that] require demonstration of teaching ability" was ranked among the top 10 institutional practices in terms of its capacity to contribute to the improvement of teaching (Wright and O'Neil 1994, p. 10).

A "disciplinary teaching colloquium" or a "pedagogical colloquium" would provide an opportunity during the interview process for a candidate "to do something that begins to demonstrate [his or her] understanding of the teaching of [the] discipline" (Shulman 1995, p. 7). Three models have been proposed for this colloquium. The first is a "course narrative or course argument" approach, in which the candidate uses a syllabus to explain how he or she would teach the course, what would be studied, and what the teacher and students would experience—thereby unveiling the candidate's philosophies of teaching and learning in the discipline. The second approach is a "colloquium centered on an essential idea or concept," in which the candidate selects one disciplinary concept that is well known to be very difficult for students to learn and explains various approaches he or she would use to promote learning of that concept. In the third approach, a "dilemma-centered colloquium," the candidate is asked to think out loud about an inherent problem in teaching the discipline, such as "the right balance between breadth and depth in an introductory course" (pp. 7–8).

The pedagogical colloquium model has been used at Georgetown University. In the German Department, for example, the course narrative and dilemma-centered approaches are introduced during the interview to encourage candidates to talk about how they would teach an introductory course. The associate vice chancellor for academic affairs at the university justifies the university's use of the pedagogical colloquium approach: "[We especially] needed to know more about what these candidates could contribute to a campus that prides itself, I think quite correctly, on quality teaching" (Byrnes 1995, p. 7).

In the end, we found ourselves thinking how much more certain we could be about having chosen the right candidate to be our future colleague by our close attention to teaching in that pivotal moment that hiring is in any department (Byrnes 1995, p. 10).

Frequent interaction, collaboration, and community among faculty

Institutional and departmental cultures that support teaching are characterized by opportunities for frequent interaction among faculty regarding teaching-related issues (Ferren 1989; Massy, Wilger, and Colbeck 1994; Wright and O'Neil 1994). Interviews of 88 faculty at six research universities indicate that one of the important institutional characteristics that can help increase the intrinsic rewards of teaching is the availability of "opportunities to talk about teaching"; in discussions with peers as well as students, faculty are able to remind themselves of the intrinsic rewards of teaching (Froh, Menges, and Walker 1993, p. 93). The results of an 11-campus study of "institutional efforts to create and/or maintain positive teaching climates" demonstrate that one of the most important characteristics of a positive teaching culture is the opportunity for collegial interaction and collaboration about teaching (LaCelle-Peterson and Finkelstein 1993, p. 22):

> *Frequently, faculty report these interactions in the context of team teaching. . . . Faculty who had taught in such course clusters . . . report that the experience was the occasion for their most meaningful teaching interactions* (LaCelle-Peterson and Finkelstein 1993, p. 28).

A relatively recent review of the literature on faculty collaboration in teaching identifies three major benefits to teachers: improvement of teaching ability, increased intellectual stimulation, and reduction in the degree of isolation associated with traditional teaching (Austin and Baldwin 1991, pp. 41–43).

After the original three-year funding period for universities participating in the Lilly Endowment's Teaching Fellows Program ended, many of the universities continued to fund the program without external support. A comprehensive evaluative study of these programs reveals that one of the characteristics of the campus cultures that fostered the continuation of such programs was the substantial sense of community that had been established among faculty associated with the program in previous years. It was customary to make clear to new teaching fellows that they were "joining a group of faculty committed to teaching and spanning university departments and years of involvement in the program" (Austin 1990b, p. 72). The creation of a community of teachers such as this has demonstrated the potential to defend "the program if budget constraints threaten its existence" (p. 72).

Whether through peer visits, informal study groups, conferences, or social events, the input of others offers new and original ideas, provides intellectual stimulation around teaching issues, and creates a sense of community that helps to break down the isolation felt by many college teachers (Aitken and Sorcinelli 1994).

A faculty development program or campus teaching center

Campus cultures that value teaching are characterized by extensive faculty development programs (LaCelle-Peterson and Finkelstein 1993; Rice and Austin 1990; Richardson 1993), often coordinated by the staff of a campus teaching center (Aitken and Sorcinelli 1994; Ambrose 1995; Austin 1990b; Fenton 1991; Jenrette and Napoli 1994; Wright and O'Neil 1994). A typical campus teaching center is a university-funded branch of the office of academic affairs. It is commonly operated by a director and trained teaching consultants. The tasks performed by the Center for Teaching at the University of Massachusetts at Amherst, for example, are representative of those performed by most centers.

Since its inception, the center has offered an ever-increasing range of resources and programs for enhancing teaching and learning. They include individual consultations, departmental consultations, workshops, seminars, conferences, teaching assistant training programs, annual award programs [like] the Teaching Fellows Program and Faculty Grants for Teaching, materials on teaching development, and institutional participation in grants and research on teaching and faculty development (Aitken and Sorcinelli 1994, p. 66).

In a recent survey, faculty development professionals ranked a "[campus teaching] center to promote effective instruction" as one of the top 10 institutional practices in terms of its capacity to improve teaching (Wright and O'Neil

1994, p. 10). A recent case study of the development of the University Teaching Center at Carnegie-Mellon University reveals a number of ways in which it "has had a marked effect on the culture of the university" (Ambrose 1995, p. 88). Support for the center persisted through a major change in the central administration; moreover, the most recent president created a new senior academic administrative position in charge of "innovation in undergraduate education," and the university "created the Center for Innovation in Learning" as a focus for research connected to the work of the teaching center (p. 88). Because of the center's success as the campus forum for discussion of issues related to teaching, this function has been expanded and included in the regular activities of other campus institutions. Recently, the center was moved to a new and prominent campus location, symbolizing "to the campus community the ever-increasing importance of teaching" at the university (p. 88). Every semester the rate of faculty participation in the center's activities has continued to increase.

Supportive and effective department chairs
Recent empirical work offers strong support for the earlier conviction of higher education scholars (particularly Lucas 1989, 1990, 1994) that one of the most critical characteristics of institutional and departmental cultures that value teaching is the presence and activities of supportive and effective department chairs. A recent qualitative investigation of the characteristics of departmental cultures that either support or inhibit faculty's efforts to work toward effective teaching included interviews with nearly 300 faculty at eight research universities, four doctoral universities, and three liberal arts colleges (Massy, Wilger, and Colbeck 1994). This ongoing study of faculty across humanities, social sciences, and science departments reveals that a supportive department chair is of pivotal importance in creating a culture that really values teaching.

> *The chair may well represent the single most important factor in determining whether or not a department actively supports teaching. Interviewees cited the crucial role the chair plays in creating an environment conducive to effective teaching. In two departments, the current chair is credited with revolutionary changes in*

One of the most critical characteristics of institutional and departmental cultures that value teaching is the presence and activities of supportive and effective department chairs.

*the department—with resolving long-standing issues
related to undergraduate education. . . . As one faculty
member said, "Faculty never moved away from their
commitment to teaching —it just wasn't rewarded as
seriously as research. [The chair] wants the quality of
both [teaching and research] to improve and has tried
to revitalize and reemphasize teaching"* (Massy, Wilger,
and Colbeck 1994, pp. 17–18).

A national sample of faculty development professionals
recently ranked "[deans'] and chairpersons' recognition of
teaching as an important aspect of academic responsibility"
in the top 10 institutional practices in terms of its potential
to improve teaching; they ranked this role of the supportive
chair second out of a possible 36 institutional practices
(Wright and O'Neil 1994, p. 15). Studies of both liberal arts
colleges and research universities show that the department
chair is essential in a campus culture that supports teaching:

*Department chairs can convey to faculty members infor-
mation about how teaching efforts are valued, how time
is most profitably allocated, and on what basis rewards
are determined. . . . Without the support of department
chairs, many incentives to encourage good teaching
may be fruitless* (Rice and Austin 1990, p. 39).

A connection between rigorous evaluation of teaching and decisions about tenure and promotion

A number of recent case studies of institutions with campus
cultures that value teaching have consistently demonstrated
that a common and outstanding characteristic of such cultures is the rigorous (peer and student) evaluation of teaching and the connection of this evaluation with decisions
about tenure and promotion (Armour 1995; Jenrette and
Napoli 1994; Richardson 1993). In a recent international
survey of faculty development professionals in the United
States (N = 165), Canada (N = 51), the United Kingdom (N =
82), and Australasia (N = 33), respondents in each sample
country and region ranked "recognition of teaching in
tenure and promotion decisions" as the number one institutional practice in terms of its "potential to improve the quality of teaching" (Wright and O'Neil 1995, pp. 12–13). Clearly,
those who probably know the most about teaching cultures

at colleges and universities around the world have in common the perception that the quality of teaching is particularly likely to be enhanced in campus cultures where the evaluation of teaching is connected to decisions about tenure and promotion (p. 18).

Further, interviews with 300 faculty on 15 campuses reveal that departmental cultures that support quality teaching are more likely to value rigorous peer and student evaluation of teaching and to connect such evaluation to decisions about tenure and promotion. According to one faculty member:

> We are scrupulous in promotion and tenure decisions about the evaluation of teaching. We insist that teaching be very good. We review faculty members on a set schedule. Assistant professors are reviewed every two years, associates every five years, and full professors every seven years. The review includes both teaching and research, as well as service and other contributions to the field (Massy, Wilger, and Colbeck 1994, pp. 16–17).

Even at research universities, departments with cultures that support teaching differ from others in important ways.

> These departments scrutinize their junior members' teaching skills and offer guidance and assistance before crucial decision points. They are changing the standard line, "Good teaching can't help you, but only terrible teaching can hurt you," to "Good (not necessarily excellent) teaching is a necessary but not sufficient condition for tenure" (Massy, Wilger, and Colbeck 1994, p. 17).

In sum, strategies to improve instruction are both nurtured by and help to create more supportive teaching cultures on college and university campuses. Supportive teaching cultures facilitate the informative feedback to teachers so important to improving teaching—feedback that comes from the teachers themselves as reflective practitioners, from students, and from colleagues, consultants, and department chairs. The next three sections consider these various sources of informative feedback and the strategies of instructional improvement associated with them.

THE TEACHER AS REFLECTIVE PRACTITIONER

*There is dissatisfaction with much of the instruction
now going on in American colleges and universities.
Criticisms of teachers and teaching have come from
legislators, students, college administrators, and even
from some faculty members. . . . A frequently offered
remedy is to make effective teaching the basis for faculty promotions. There are those who believe that teaching will be improved only if it is somehow evaluated
and used as a criterion for appointments or promotions. This may be true, but . . . if course or instructional improvement is the goal, something more than a
single good-bad judgment is needed—something that
will give a teacher the kind of specific information
needed for improvement* (Centra 1972, p. 1).

Nearly a quarter century after those remarks were written,
the quest for discovering "ways in which college teaching is
being and can be improved" (Centra 1972, p. 1) remains.
This section and the next two examine the recent and some
of the earlier literature on the subject, emphasizing the theoretical and empirical foundations underlying the success of
contemporary strategies for improving instruction.

Researchers and analysts consistently have demonstrated,
both theoretically and empirically, that college professors are
primarily motivated by the intrinsic rewards of academic
work, including intrinsic rewards gained from teaching
(Austin and Gamson 1983; Berman and Skeff 1988; Bess 1977;
Froh, Menges, and Walker 1993; McKeachie 1979, 1982; Olsen
1993). Intrinsically motivated individuals usually want to feel
competent and have a sense of self-determination—two
needs that are closely related if not intertwined. In fact, it is
"the need for self-determined competence" that underlies
intrinsic motivation (Deci and Ryan 1985, p. 32). "This basic
need leads people to situations and activities that interest
them, that provide optimal challenges, that allow them to
learn and achieve" (Deci and Ryan 1982, p. 28). The need for
self-determined competence also prompts individuals to scan
the environment for feedback that informs them of the results
of their performance—producing a critical psychological state
that an intrinsically motivated person continuously seeks
through work (Hackman and Oldham 1976). Teachers, for
example, might:

*. . . develop instructional routines that include teaching,
reflection on information about successes and failures,
and then teaching again, with attempts to make
changes based on feedback. . . . Many college teachers
do this naturally. They solicit information as feedback;
they reflect on their expectations, beliefs, and values;
and they experiment with different ways of teaching*
(Menges 1991, p. 27).

The informative feedback that intrinsically motivated professors continuously seek is exactly what drives the process
of instructional improvement. Further, most strategies for
improving instruction can be meaningfully arranged into
categories according to the primary source of informative
feedback that serves to initiate, direct, and/or sustain the
changes in instructional behavior associated with a particular
strategy. The most prominent sources of such feedback (as
distinguished from "methods" for obtaining this feedback)
are widely discussed in the literature on the evaluation of
teaching—*self, students, colleagues, consultants,* and *chairs*
(Braskamp and Ory 1994; Centra 1993). Indeed, the attention given to the usefulness of feedback from these sources
for the improvement of teaching relative to personnel decisions has increased noticeably in the past 10 to 15 years
(Braskamp, Brandenburg, and Ory 1984; Centra 1979). This
section and the next two discuss strategies for improving
instruction that depend particularly on informative feedback
from one of these five sources. This section focuses on
strategies that rely on instructors themselves as the primary
source of informative feedback to promote improvement; it
views the teacher as a reflective practitioner.

Practice-Centered Inquiry
The first source of informative feedback available to most
instructors is themselves. And the first information many
instructors receive about their teaching comes from their
own observations of their teaching, coupled with their
reflections on those observations. Instructional improvement,
whether at the remedial, facilitative, or optimizing level, is
best accomplished "in a manner that will permit careful
monitoring" (Sullivan 1985, p. 77). One way to create a continuous source of informative feedback is to supplement the
traditional adage, "Think before you act," with the less con-

ventional, "Act and reflect on your action" (Argyris, Putnam, and Smith 1985, p. 52). Because college professors often strongly need to seek self-determined competence by continuously scanning their instructional environment for informative feedback, their behavior can be examined and the source of changes in their behavior understood by viewing them as "reflective practitioners" (Schon 1983, 1987). College teachers, like most professionals, face familiar situations repetitively. Some aspects of their behaviors and practices become routinized and automatic; portions of their understandings become tacit and therefore remain unexamined. But routine classroom practices sometimes produce unexpected outcomes. Teachers can respond to surprises, of course, by ignoring them, but often surprises in the classroom stimulate reflection. If a professor thinks reflectively about an episode of teaching after class, he or she engages in "reflection-on-action," but if he or she thinks reflectively about a teaching episode while in the midst of it, he or she engages in "reflection-in-action." While reflection-on-action could lead to instructional change tomorrow, reflection-in-action makes on-the-spot changes possible.

College teachers form personal, implicit theories of teaching upon which they often depend, even though they are not particularly aware of their theories. Such theories are likely to be inaccurate because they are developed more or less implicitly or subconsciously rather than explicitly and thoughtfully. The purpose of these implicit theories is largely to protect instructors from the ambiguity and complexity of the teaching environment; further, they are influenced by cultural norms grounded in the broader institutional setting of higher education (Rando and Menges 1991). Interview data from qualitative studies have shown that such personal theories do indeed influence teaching behaviors (Fox 1983; Menges and Rando 1989). It is important to reflect on turning these theories into opportunities for improving instruction:

When we reflect on our experience, our implicit theories become apparent, even transparent. Having been explicated, implicit theories and the behaviors they produce become part of what we can think about and experience directly. We are then able to use these theories productively, perhaps in combination with more formal theories. They become vehicles for improving our practice,

rather than mere determinants of our reflexive behavior
(Rando and Menges 1991, p. 11).

College teachers make certain assumptions about their
teaching situations that manifest themselves in particular
values and standards. A teacher's behaviors are generally
intended to produce consequences that are consistent with
those values and standards. In a particular teaching situation,
informative feedback about these immediate consequences
allows the teacher to assess his or her effectiveness. If a
discrepancy is detected between consequences and values
or standards, teachers can engage in a "reflective conversation with the situation" (Schon 1983, p. 163). This reflection-
in-action can help teachers to become more aware of
differences between what they say they do (espoused theories) and what they actually do (theories-in-use) in a particular teaching situation (Argyris, Putnam, and Smith 1985, pp.
81– 82). This type of "practice-centered inquiry" (Chism and
Sanders 1986, p. 57) can lead reflective teachers to change
more than just those behaviors or strategies intended to satisfy the assumptions, values, or standards currently held
about the teaching situation. Reflective teachers can go a
step farther and raise questions about the appropriateness or
validity of those underlying assumptions, values, or standards that in effect "govern" their teaching behavior in a
particular situation. In short, in-depth knowledge or "double-
loop learning" underlies effective teaching in a given situation (Argyris, Putnam, and Smith 1985, p. 86).

Recently, critically reflective teaching (Brookfield 1995)
and transformative theories of adult learning and development (M. Clark 1993; Mezirow 1991) have been applied to
the process of instructional improvement. In the first stage of
transformative learning, actions that generate informative
feedback help instructors to increase their awareness of (and
make explicit) the assumptions and beliefs they hold about
a teaching situation. During the second stage, instructors
study informative feedback regarding the sources and consequences of their assumptions and beliefs. In the third stage,
informative feedback begins to challenge instructors' basic
beliefs and assumptions. This stage is characterized by "critical self-reflection" that can be carried out in "discourse with
others" or "through 'discourse' with oneself (for example, in
journal writing)" (Cranton 1994). The last stage of transfor-

mative learning involves instructors' revising their basic assumptions about a teaching situation and developing plans to try out new teaching behaviors, which in turn generates more informative feedback as a focus for ongoing reflection on teaching practices (pp. 739–41). Another element added to the concept of reflection is the need for teachers "to understand how considerations of power undergird, frame, and distort educational processes and interactions" (Brookfield 1995, p. 8).

Engaging in practice-centered inquiry and the attendant activities of reflective practice has been shown to be a useful strategy for improving instruction (Amundsen, Gryspeerdt, and Moxness 1993; Chism, Sanders, and Zitlow 1987; Dahlin 1994; Parker and Lawson 1978; Smith and Schwartz 1988; Stevens 1988). Activities that constitute practice-centered inquiry or reflective practice can be arranged along a continuum. At one end are the informal observations, questions, and realizations that arise in the act of teaching, coupled with the immediate reflections on them during and shortly after class. In the middle of the continuum are more persistent, yet still informal, efforts at observation and inquiry; for example, notes could be taken and records kept so that sustained reflection could yield meaningful patterns of behavior, possibly leading to a change in teaching methods. At the other end of the continuum, reflective practice takes place within the framework of a more formal research design (Chism and Sanders 1986, pp. 58–59).

A recent ethnographic study of a college professor used data from interviews, classroom observations, and documents to construct a vivid portrait of an effective reflective practitioner (Dahlin 1994). This professor's regular use of a teaching journal illustrates the kind of informal day-to-day reflective practice that makes her particularly effective:

From the beginning of her career, Margaret used a technique that ensured reflection: a professional journal in which she wrote about her teaching, learning, and growth. She grappled with her goals, practices, and persona, interspersing contemplation with information. An entry on September 29, 1983, demonstrated the intertwining of theory, practice, and introspection: "We corrected each other's quizzes as a way of reinforcing knowledge and getting students to open up and talk in front of each other. General mayhem ensued compared to usual silence. Fine with me. We all need to relax more, trust ourselves with each other, take risks of exposing ourselves." Margaret related the activity (correcting quizzes), offered a rationale (a way of reinforcing knowledge and getting students to open up), and reflected on its value as she saw it ("We all need to relax more."). Again and again, Margaret's journal showed a person operating simultaneously in these three spheres. She described her practice, her reasoning, and her current reaction (Dahlin 1994, p. 59).

Other research has been designed to promote reflection about one's teaching and to study the outcome of this reflection. For example, in the Teaching Excellence Program at Ohio State University, 17 faculty members from a wide variety of fields carried out one or more semester-long practice-centered inquiry "projects" (both formal and informal) designed to encourage experimentation and reflection on different ways to improve their courses and teaching. Over the course of 15 biweekly seminars, participants were able to share reflections about their projects in a "safe" environment (Chism, Sanders, and Zitlow 1987). Although the researchers were concerned that many of the faculty did not really examine their teaching "critically" and that inquiry projects did not generate "long-term growth in teaching understandings" (pp. 14–15), they nevertheless outlined certain overall positive results of the projects:

Four kinds of results of the completed projects were noted: immediate improvements in practice, justification of existing practices, professional publication/presentation, and acquisition of general knowledge. . . . The 14 [projects] that led to immediate improvements in practice are exemplified by projects in which new teaching techniques were tested or materials were developed (Chism, Sanders, and Zitlow 1987, p. 12).

In another study, sponsored by the Professional and Organizational Network in Higher Education, faculty participants in a three-day workshop were asked to reflect on their teaching and to make explicit the theories of action guiding their teaching. Each participant wrote a case study of an actual problem that had occurred in their teaching, including any strategies they had used, any barriers encountered, and a record of their conversations with students that showed what was actually spoken as well as any thoughts or feelings withheld. Participants then shared these reflections with other workshop participants (Smith and Schwartz 1988). The researchers believe they "were successful in getting the participants to *recognize* and *accept* their action strategies of making attributions and evaluations without illustrating or testing them, and of behaving as if [they] were true." They agreed that in the future, however, they would also focus on "identification (and change) of the *underlying values* of the theory-in-use that informs these counterproductive strategies and holds them in place" (p. 82).

. . . most instructional change does not comprise sweeping innovations . . .

At McGill University, faculty met weekly for two years in a number of discussion groups (Amundsen, Gryspeerdt, and Moxness 1993). Weekly meetings typically consisted of activities that encouraged participants to reflect on the application of new teaching principles and practices in their own courses. Participants then shared reflections with faculty colleagues in a supportive environment. At the end of the two-year period, the great majority of participants either already had used or planned to experiment with the new teaching approaches discussed in the seminars, and several participants carried out formal classroom research projects.

> *We predicted that these methods would support the central premise of practice-centered inquiry, namely, that a large part of a professor's knowledge about teaching evolves from reflection and experimentation. The content of the faculty discussions and the number of professors who actually tried various teaching approaches suggest that the faculty discussion group structure is appropriate in addressing the more informal levels of reflection and experimentation* (Amundsen, Gryspeerdt, and Moxness 1993, p. 350).

It is of some interest that a qualitative study of the highly personal and individual nature of instructional changes carried out by 12 full-time faculty reveals that most instructional change does not comprise sweeping innovations; instead, "professors recalled gradually evolving techniques within one aspect of teaching . . . [by] 'tinkering' with instructional strategies" (Stevens 1988, p. 67). The interview data provide a somewhat different perspective on the nature, importance, and effectiveness of reflective practice by illustrating two different types of tinkering—reactive and reflective. Reactive tinkerers tended to consider a limited range of teaching techniques and to seek simple solutions to instructional problems in ways that were unrelated to any meaningful analysis of what would best help their students learn. Reflective tinkerers considered a wider range of teaching techniques because they continuously experimented with and modified instructional techniques according to a meaningful analysis of what would help their students learn.

Self-Assessment

The ultimate foundation of all reflective practice or self-reflection is the ability and opportunity to engage in self-evaluation or self-assessment. Self-assessment has certain distinctive properties and advantages: Much of it is done more or less automatically; it is the most immediate source of information about one's teaching; immediate adjustments can be made in response to it; it is self-generated and therefore optimally meaningful to the individual instructor; and compared to all other sources of information, it takes place the most continuously (Fink 1995, p. 193). Some form of self-confrontation is a natural prerequisite for enhancing self-awareness of one's effectiveness in teaching. A recent book, *Assessing Faculty Work,* justifies the importance of self-assessment:

> *Faculty themselves are the most important assessment source because only they can provide descriptions of their work, the thinking behind it, and their own personal reporting, appraisals, interpretations, and goals. Self-assessment involves reflection and judgment. Only the professors themselves can make a case for their work. In fact, we have stressed that campuses should support a culture of assessment in which faculty continuously monitor and assess their own progress* (Braskamp and Ory 1994, p. 102).

Two common methods of collecting self-evaluations are self-rating forms and self-reports (Carroll 1981). At many colleges and universities, faculty are asked to complete the same (or slightly reworded) teaching evaluation questionnaire as their students. This approach enables faculty to analyze their work and to reflect on their teaching behaviors along the same dimensions their students use to evaluate them. A meta-analysis of 19 studies found that the correlation across instructors (which indicates the extent of *relative* similarity) between instructors' overall self-ratings and their students' overall ratings of them was +.29—a statistically significant but modest positive correlation (Feldman 1989). In terms of the extent of *absolute* similarity of ratings, however, instructors on average tended to rate themselves at a level similar to their students' ratings. In combination, these two sets of findings indicate that some instructors rated themselves more favorably and some less favorably than their students, accounting for the modest correlation coefficient. In terms of *profile* similarity—the pattern of ratings of more effective and less effective teaching behaviors—the average correlation for 10 pertinent studies evaluated was a robust +.84, "indicating that teachers as a group assess their relative strengths and weaknesses in ways highly similar to current students as a group" (p. 153). This particular finding provides evidence of validity for self-ratings as a means by which instructors can accurately identify the relative strengths and weaknesses in their teaching. Another meta-analysis, of 31 studies, found that the average correlation between teachers and students in terms of the importance they attached to the contribution of various teaching behaviors to effective teaching was +.71 (Feldman 1988). This finding offers a possible resolution to the often-disputed claim that students and their instructors disagree on what constitutes good teaching; it also offers indirect support for the validity of self-evaluations.

Other evidence suggests that faculty who have not experienced course evaluations (for example, because no campus system for evaluation exists or because instructors are teaching a course for the first time) are more likely to rate themselves higher than their students do (Centra 1973b). This finding provides yet another reason for the importance of conducting regular self-ratings. Further, some research indicates that the greater the positive discrepancy—the amount by which self-ratings exceed students' ratings—at midterm, the more likely the instructor will improve teaching behaviors, as evidenced by increases in end-of-term ratings by students (Centra 1973a; Pambookian 1976).

The Teaching Portfolio

Self-reports completed by college professors traditionally have been limited to vitae and reports of activities. Recently, however, they have been conceptually and functionally expanded into a medium, compendium, and showcase for reflective practice—namely, the teaching portfolio (Edgerton, Hutchings, and Quinlan 1991; Seldin 1991). Teaching portfolios are essentially an elaborate and reflective form of self-evaluation (Kahn 1993). The idea of the *teaching* portfolio is borrowed from the long tradition among architects, photographers, painters, and other artists of constructing portfolios of one's best work. In the United States, use of the teaching portfolio has grown geometrically: The number of colleges and universities using teaching portfolios (in one form or another) grew from an estimated 10 institutions in 1990 to about 500 institutions in 1995 (Seldin, Annis, and Zubizarreta 1995, p. 238).[*]

The use of teaching portfolios came earlier to Canadian universities, which have been using "teaching dossiers" since the early 1980s. To assist institutions with this work, the Canadian Association of University Teachers, in conjunction with the Center for Teaching and Learning Services at McGill University, published a comprehensive set of guidelines for preparation and use of the dossier (Shore, Foster, Knapper, Nadeau, Neill, and Sim 1986). Briefly, a teaching dossier is "a summary of a professor's major teaching accomplishments and strengths. It is to a professor's teaching what lists of publications, grants, and academic honors are to research" (p. 1). The guidelines suggest three broad categories of items that might be included in the dossier: (1) *the products*

---

[*]Readers interested in learning more about (or constructing) teaching portfolios have several sources of information. Seldin (1991, 1993) provides sample teaching portfolios from a wide variety of disciplines and types of colleges and universities. Anderson (1993) describes, in some detail, the use of teaching portfolios at 25 different colleges and universities, including illustrative exhibits and names and addresses of campus representatives to contact for more information. Richlin and Manning (1995) present a detailed curriculum to guide faculty and administrators in the construction of course portfolios (see also Cerbin 1994), teaching portfolios, and the development of a peer review and evaluation-of-teaching system.

of good teaching, such as students' test scores, workbooks, logs, reports of field work, or evidence of effective thesis supervision; (2) *material from oneself,* such as courses taught, enrollments, course materials, research on one's teaching, instructional innovations, or course development; and (3) *information from others,* such as data from students' evaluations, written evaluations or interviews of students, statements from colleagues who have observed one's teaching, or statements about teaching from administrators (pp. 10–11). Finally, the guidelines provide 49 detailed items for possible inclusion (with a description, rationale, and example for each). Two important items that are known to be commonly used in teaching portfolios (see Seldin 1991) are not on this detailed list, however: a "reflective statement by the professor describing personal teaching philosophy, strategies, and objectives" and a "personal statement by the professor describing teaching goals for the next five years" (p. 10). A statement of teaching goals is among the items appearing most frequently in more than 400 portfolios reviewed (Seldin 1993, p. 6).

Conceptually, a good teaching portfolio should contain several items.

> *At the heart of the portfolio as we envision it are* samples of teaching performance: *not just what teachers say about their practice but artifacts and examples of what they actually do. We argue, too, that portfolios should be* reflective: *work samples would be accompanied by faculty commentary and explanation that reveal not only what was done but why, the thinking behind the teaching. Finally, we argue for portfolios that are . . . a careful selection of evidence organized around agreed-upon categories, which themselves represent key dimensions of the scholarship of teaching* (Edgerton, Hutchings, and Quinlan 1991, p. 4).

Unlike most other strategies for improving instruction, teaching portfolios provide opportunities for professors to *reflect* on their own teaching within the *content* of their own disciplines and within the *context* of their own particular classes. Thus, the concept of a teaching portfolio is based squarely on the notion of viewing a teacher as a *reflective practitioner* (Schon 1983). In the process of constructing a portfolio, professors must engage again and again in "reflective conversation with a [teaching] situation" in coming to grips with both the nature (the what) of their teaching and the thinking (the why) behind that teaching (p. 163). Typically, each entry in a portfolio is related in some way to a sample of teaching work and/or the teacher's reflections on and explanations of that sample. The evidence of teaching (work samples) and the professor's reflections on that evidence are also grounded in the pedagogical content knowledge associated with teaching one's own disciplinary content within the context of one's own classes (Shulman 1986, 1987, 1989). The experiences of participants in Stanford's Teacher Assessment Project reveal that:

> *[General] reflection, divorced from evidence of actual performance, fails to capture the situated nature of teaching. Work samples alone aren't intelligible. But work samples plus reflection make a powerful formula. The reflection is "grounded" by being connected to a particular instance of teaching; the work sample is made meaningful and placed in context through reflection* (Edgerton, Hutchings, and Quinlan 1991, p. 9).

Apparently no experimental research has been conducted to investigate whether or not teaching portfolios contribute systematically to the improvement of instruction or whether the use of teaching portfolios is associated with any of the traditional measures of effective instruction, such as students' achievement or students' ratings of teaching. What is available are the reports from numerous faculty respondents that their teaching has improved because of the construction of a teaching portfolio (Hutchings 1993a; Seldin 1993; Seldin, Annis, and Zubizarreta 1995). Additionally, faculty developers who coordinate and appraise campus activities related to teaching portfolios are consistently affirmative in their belief that teaching portfolios promote improved instruction (Anderson 1993; Seldin 1991; Seldin and Annis 1990).

One of the earliest, best-documented, and most successful tests of the use of teaching portfolios for improving instruction was at Ball State University in 1990. Twenty faculty members were randomly selected from over 100 who volunteered to construct teaching portfolios. The responses of faculty members and faculty developers regarding the positive impact of teaching portfolios on teaching at Ball State are representative of the assessments of their counterparts at other colleges and universities. The project had several successful outcomes:

> *The quality of portfolios was quite high. If there was one recurring comment from the participants, it was their common enjoyment in the project. Some found it refreshing to discover from the completed portfolio just how effective they have been in the classroom. Others found the focused thinking on teaching effectiveness a stimulus for self-improvement* (Seldin and Annis 1990, p. 200).

But beyond these outcomes, the coordinators learned something else:

> *Virtually all participating professors acknowledged that in the process of collecting documents and materials they were forced to rethink their teaching strategies and goals. They asked themselves* why *they do* what *they do in the classroom. That alone induced many faculty to engage colleagues in discussion about teaching and to sharpen their own classroom performance* (Seldin 1991, p. 29).

The Teaching Culture, Instructional Change, and Reflective Practice

As we analyze various ways that teachers use reflective practice to generate informative feedback, we do not want to lose sight of potential connections with elements of the teaching culture and the mechanisms that characterize the three stages of the process of instructional change. The following example shows the relevance of certain elements of a supportive teaching culture and discusses the *unfreezing* phase of the process of instructional change (see figure 1 on p. 17). Examples for the changing and refreezing phases appear in later sections.

Suppose the faculty senate and the office of the vice chancellor for academic affairs have recently collaborated to establish a uniform system for evaluating faculty in which teachers are to be reviewed by peers using portfolios, with the rating of the portfolio to be weighted equally with research in subsequent decisions about tenure and promotion. Consider a tenured faculty member who is applying for the rank of full professor. During the process of drafting the "statement of teaching philosophy" for her portfolio, she has difficulty developing a strong rationale for her predominantly lecture-style approach to teaching. Over the years she has developed an expressive and stimulating style of lecturing, and she views herself as an "innovative" teacher who strives to maximize students' learning. She knows, however, that research now shows that students learn more in an active than in a passive role. The idea of active learning makes her think about the problem-solving groups that the department chair—who is already a full professor—has been using in a similar class. She has heard students talk about what the chair has students do in the problem-solving groups, and she considers this approach very innovative.

In this scenario, the primary source of information for changing the method of instruction comes from self-reflection. Additionally, several elements of a supportive teaching culture are at work: high-level administrative commitment to the value of quality teaching, faculty members' involvement and sense of ownership in the planning and implementation of activities to improve teaching, a broader definition of scholarship to include teaching, and a connection between rigorous evaluation of teaching and decisions involving tenure and promotion. Finally, the mechanisms of the unfreezing stage of change are present. *Disconfirmation* occurs when the professor tries to justify her approach, *comparison* when her current teaching practices do not meet her innovative teaching standards, and *safety* in the idea of trying the chair's problem-solving groups. If this professor, like many others, strongly needs to be competent and to engage in self-determination, these factors are likely to generate a motivation to change.

LISTENING TO THE VOICE OF STUDENTS

By far the most common method used to evaluate the quality of teaching among colleges and universities in North America is "formal student ratings, usually obtained by means of a standardized, objectively scored evaluation form" (Murray 1984, p. 118). A number of surveys have studied the availability of ratings by students at a wide variety of different types of public and private institutions. Student ratings were collected and available as a source of diagnostic feedback for instructional improvement at over 80 percent of 756 institutions surveyed in 1976 (Centra 1979). In a 1985 study, student ratings of teaching were available at over 95 percent of 630 institutions surveyed (Erickson 1986). A 1989 survey of professional faculty developers (one per institution) reveals that 99 percent of the 155 institutions in the survey either reported widespread use of or planned to use student ratings of instruction for the assessment and improvement of teaching (Kurfiss and Boice 1990).

Student Ratings and the Improvement of Instruction

But have student ratings of teaching led to the improvement of college teaching? Some researchers (see, e.g., Marsh 1987; Marsh and Dunkin 1992; Murray 1987b) argue that logically they should.

> *The logical case for student instructional ratings is that since they incorporate evaluative functions that have been found to improve performance in other contexts, such ratings would be expected to improve teaching similarly. For one thing, student ratings provide informative feedback useful for diagnosing instructional strengths. Second, feedback from students can provide the impetus for professional development activities aimed at improved teaching. Third, use of student ratings in salary, promotion, and tenure decisions gives faculty members a tangible incentive for putting time and effort into improvement of teaching. Finally, use of student ratings in tenure and retention decisions provides a selection mechanism whereby better teachers are more likely to be retained by the institution. There are good reasons, then, for expecting that student ratings should lead to improved teaching, particularly if used for both summative and formative purposes* (Murray 1987b, p. 3).

Where the quality of teaching has improved over the years, can it be attributed to the impact of feedback from student ratings? Some positive evidence that it is comes from seven surveys of college teachers (all but one conducted during the 1980s), which asked whether student ratings had provided useful feedback for improving instruction and whether student ratings had led to improved teaching. Results of the seven surveys in combination reveal that about 67 percent of the faculty stated that student ratings were useful and about 80 percent stated that such ratings led to improved teaching (Murray 1987b).

Experimental research on this issue has focused primarily on whether informative feedback from student ratings (including written comments by students) received at midterm are associated with higher end-of-term ratings for those receiving feedback, compared to a control group of faculty receiving no midterm feedback. This research was reviewed several times between 1980 and 1990. An examination of changes in student ratings of teaching as a result of the faculty's receiving feedback on student ratings alone, student ratings plus consultation, and discrepancies between self-ratings and student ratings concludes that "feedback from students can positively affect subsequent teaching, particularly if ratings are accompanied by consultation. Faculty most likely to change are those whose student ratings are less positive than their self-ratings and they are probably the persons [in] whom consultants' efforts should be invested" (Levinson-Rose and Menges 1981, pp. 419–20).

The first actual meta-analysis of the results of experimental studies of the effect of feedback from student ratings on improving instruction examined 22 comparisons based on 17 studies. The average effect of feedback from student ratings on end-of-term ratings was a statistically significant but modest increase of +.38 standard deviation. For the specific instructional dimension of skill in delivery, the average effect was +.47 standard deviation. The effect of feedback from student ratings without consultation was +.20 standard deviation, and the effect of student feedback with consultation was +.64 standard deviation (Cohen 1980). A more recent meta-analysis evaluated 31 comparisons from 27 studies and found the average effect of feedback from student ratings on end-of-term ratings to be +.44 standard deviation. The effect of feedback from student ratings without consultation was

+.22 standard deviation, and the effect of student feedback with consultation was +1.1 standard deviations (Menges and Brinko 1986). In the most recent meta-analysis of such experimental studies, the average effect of feedback from student ratings on end-of-term ratings was an increase of +.342 standard deviation (L'Hommedieu, Menges, and Brinko 1990). After identifying a variety of methodological limitations (threats to the internal or external validity) of the studies they evaluated, the researchers drew the following conclusions in support of the positive effects of feedback from student ratings on improved instruction:

> *The literature reveals a persistently positive, albeit small, effect from written feedback alone and a considerably increased effect when written feedback is augmented with personal consultation. The threats we have discussed operate in almost every case to attenuate rather than to exaggerate feedback effects. We expect that improved research will document effects that are more substantial and robust than those shown so far* (L'Hommedieu, Menges, and Brinko 1990, p. 240).

Several observations are noteworthy about this literature. First, faculty most likely to improve in response to feedback from students may be those with larger rather than smaller discrepancies between their self-ratings and students' ratings on one or more dimensions of teaching (Centra 1973a; Levinson-Rose and Menges 1981; Pambookian 1976). It seems plausible to assume that students would rate at least one or two aspects of most professors' teaching at a level below the internal standards of performance the professors maintain. Second, evidence based on logical argument and faculty surveys (Murray 1987b) and on experimental research consistently shows that feedback from student ratings can be of value in improving one's instructional effectiveness. Third, the importance of consultation in enhancing the effects of feedback from student ratings on the quality of teaching is notable (Cohen 1980; L'Hommedieu, Menges, and Brinko 1990; Marsh and Roche 1993; Menges and Brinko 1986). The literature in this area emphasizes the utility of sitting down with a colleague or teaching consultant to jointly interpret the feedback, select targets for improvement, and develop strategies for instructional change. (The literature on effec-

. . . faculty most likely to improve in response to feedback from students may be those with larger rather than smaller discrepancies between their self-ratings and students' ratings . . .

tive models of instructional consultation is considered in the next section, "Colleagues, Consultants, and Chairs.")

Another interesting approach to using feedback from student ratings to improve instruction addresses the need for a consultant in a creative way. This approach is based on the distinctive work done in the study of specific (low-inference) behavior of teachers, as opposed to the more standard (global or high-inference) teaching behaviors (Murray 1987a). Research on specific, low-inference behaviors can be related to experiments on the effects of students' ratings:

> *In most of these experiments, midterm feedback consist-ed of mean student ratings of global instructor charac-teristics [like] "clarity," "rapport," and "overall effectiveness." Low ratings on items of this sort inform the teacher that something is wrong but provide no indication of the specific classroom behaviors that gave rise to the problem or the specific changes that will bring about improvement. On the other hand, low rat-ings on specific behavioral items [like] "maintains eye contact with students," "indicates the transition from one topic to the next," and "uses frequent examples" provide a clear signal as to what is wrong and what remedial action is needed. According to this analysis, the reason student feedback plus expert consultation produced large instructional gains is that the expert consultant was able to interpret global student ratings in specific behavioral terms and to recommend specific behavioral change strategies* (Murray 1987a, p. 89).

The results of this research can be interpreted as showing that the need for instructional consultation can be mediated somewhat by providing better diagnostic feedback to in-structors in at least two ways. First, if instructors are more knowledgeable about the specific teaching behaviors that are associated with the more global behaviors that students rate on traditional evaluation forms, professors will be better able to interpret the meaning of ratings of items found on most of these forms. Second, more appropriate diagnostic feedback forms could be constructed using specific, low-inference behavioral items "and thus provide clearer pre-scriptions for remedial action. Low ratings on items [like] 'maintains eye contact with students' . . . provide the instructor with clear signals as to what is wrong and what remedial action is needed" (Murray 1991, p. 163).

Research with specific, low-inference items has demonstrated very high interrater reliability among students (Murray 1983). These specific behavioral ratings correlate highly with students' achievement, students' motivation, and overall ratings of teachers' effectiveness (Murray 1983, 1985, 1991). Some of the specific behaviors that correlate highly with overall teaching ratings are in the dimensions of enthusiasm (e.g., "speaks expressively or emphatically," "moves about while lecturing," "gestures with hands and arms," "shows facial expressions"), clarity (e.g., "gives multiple examples," "points out practical applications," "stresses important points"), and interaction/rapport (e.g., "asks questions of class," "encourages questions and comments," "addresses students by name," "shows concern for student progress," "friendly, easy to talk to") (Murray 1985, p. 25). The categories first appeared in the Teacher Behaviors Inventory, which was originally used to provide student ratings at midterm to an experimental group of 30 teachers randomly selected from 60 participating instructors, with the remaining 30 teachers serving as the control group that did not receive feedback.[*] Feedback consisted of descriptive statistics on the ratings for each item along with brief instructions to aid in interpreting data. Both the actual gains between midterm and end-of-term ratings and the average end-of-term student ratings of amount of improvement in teaching were significantly higher for the experimental group compared to the control group, and the "effect size for [specific] behavioral feedback was .73 standard deviation units, which is considerably higher than the average effect size of .20 reported by Cohen (1980) for student feedback of a more global nature" (Murray 1991, p. 165).

Talking with Students

Various ways of listening to the voice of students have been used as the basis of different strategies for improving instruction. Faculty in one study were asked to indicate their relative preferences for student feedback collected in differ-

---

[*]The entire diagnostic version of the Teacher Behaviors Inventory (available in Murray 1987a, pp. 92–94) can be reproduced "for any valid research or instructional development purpose."

ent forms—ratings on objective questionnaire items, written comments by students, and reports of group interviews with students. For purposes of improving instruction, group interviews and written comments were rated similarly and as more accurate and more trustworthy than objective items. In terms of believability and interpretability, written comments were rated above group interviews, but both were rated higher than objective items. Group interviews with students were rated as the most comprehensive, most useful, and most valuable among all three for the purpose of improving instruction (Ory and Braskamp 1981). Similarly, students have been asked to indicate their degree of satisfaction with different processes of collecting their evaluations of teaching. Students in one study preferred group interviews to ratings forms because of the midterm "timing, quality of feedback, oral exchange of information, and personal approach involved" (Wulff, Staton-Spicer, Hess, and Nyquist 1985, p. 43). In a more recent study, students were found to prefer group interviews at midterm (and the extended reactions from instructors associated with them) more than traditional standardized ratings collected at the end of the term (Abbott, Wulff, Nyquist, Ropp, and Hess 1990).

A content analysis comparing student feedback collected through written comments on a questionnaire with feedback collected from group interviews or discussion reveals that the information acquired did not differ in terms of the unanticipated, prescriptive, detailed, elaborative, or expressive nature of the content. Both teachers and students, however, strongly preferred group discussions over questionnaires (Tiberius, Sackin, and Cappe 1987). This result is understandable, because "the discussion group data certainly contain more anecdotes, direct quotations in a conversational style, expressions of emotion, and subtle differences of opinion, all of which add liveliness and immediacy to the final report" (pp. 294–95).

Probably the most compelling justification for using group discussions or interviews in an effort to improve instruction in the classroom comes from an experimental study of the impact on feedback from end-of-term student ratings plus group discussion (without consultation), and feedback from student ratings only, compared to a control group that did not receive feedback (Tiberius, Sackin, Slingerland, Jubas, Bell, and Matlow 1989). The study examined teachers and students in the clinical setting of nine different subspecialty wards of a large university hospital. Results indicate that the "addition of a supplementary feedback method, a student group discussion technique, to feedback from student ratings resulted in a much greater improvement [in teachers'] performance than did feedback from student ratings alone. The improvement was dramatic, *and* it was sustained over successive groups of students . . ." (p. 676).

Several different ways of using interviews with students to give feedback to teachers have been reported as successful strategies for improving instruction: the group discussion (Tiberius 1988; Tiberius, Sackin, and Cappe 1987; Tiberius, Sackin, Janzen, and Preece 1993; Tiberius et al. 1989), small-group instructional diagnosis (W.E. Bennett 1987; Clark and Bekey 1979; Coffman 1991; N. Diamond 1988; Wulff et al. 1985), the class interview (Heppner and Johnston 1994; Kyger 1984), and quality control circles (Cross and Angelo 1988; Kogut 1984). One technique, often referred to as the "discussion group" (Tiberius 1988; Tiberius, Sackin, and Cappe 1987), typically begins with an initial consultation with the instructor. During this session, participants discuss the instructor's goals and means of achieving them. Next, a group of students are selected randomly from the instructor's class list for participation in a group interview led by a group facilitator other than the instructor and unknown to the students (usually a teaching consultant). During the interview, the facilitator takes notes while the students respond to broad questions about what aspects of the instructor's teaching have been helpful and should be maintained, what things have not been helpful and should be changed, and what suggestions they have regarding ways the teacher can improve the class. The facilitator then prepares a written summary of the students' anonymous comments and gives it to the instructor to read, after which they meet to discuss the comments and strategies for change. Finally, the instructor discusses selected issues with the students.

Recent innovations in this approach—now called "alliances for change"—have made it possible to use the technique without the direct involvement of an outside teaching consultant (Tiberius 1995; Tiberius et al. 1993). After participating in an initial orientation, demonstration, and training session, faculty form pairs. Teachers and their partners meet to share their teaching goals and methods, identify specific concerns about teaching, and arrange for classroom visits. Near the end of the classroom visit, the teacher introduces the partner and then leaves the room so that the partner can randomly select four to six students to form an "agenda group." The partner interviews the agenda group (whose members are unknown to the teacher), using a procedure similar to that used in the original group discussion approach (identifying teaching practices that are considered helpful as well as things that could be changed), writes a report, submits it to the teacher, and discusses the report with the teacher. At the next meeting of the class, the teacher explains what has already happened and asks the whole class to write on a sheet of paper aspects of teaching that are helpful and things that could be changed so that they can be compared with points that arose in the agenda group. At the class after that, the teacher asks for volunteers to form a "conversation group" with the teacher and partner to develop suggestions for improvement based on a report of the now-combined ideas of the agenda group and the survey of the whole class. The teacher shares the results with the class and tells them how he or she plans to address the problems. Finally, the issues raised in the agenda group's discussion are arranged into items on an end-of-term questionnaire.

Another technique for group discussion, known as "small-group instructional diagnosis" (SGID), was originally developed at the University of Washington (Clark and Bekey 1979) as an extension of one component of the clinical approach to instructional consultation earlier developed at the University of Massachusetts (Bergquist and Phillips 1977). It has been widely used and is considered substantially effective (see, e.g., W.E. Bennett 1987; Coffman 1991; Wulff et al. 1985). The process begins with a meeting between the consultant and the teacher, at which time the procedure is described and specific instructional concerns identified. Next, the consultant visits the classroom and forms groups of six to eight students. Each group chooses a recorder, who writes down only responses to the following three questions on which the group has reached consensus: "What do you like about the course?" "What would you like changed in the course?" "What suggestions do you have for improving the course?" (N. Diamond 1988, p. 90). Recorders then share these comments with the entire class. As each comment is presented, the consultant makes sure everyone understands its meaning and then asks for a show of hands indicating agreement or disagreement with the comment. The consultant then collects materials from the group and prepares a summary report for discussion with the instructor. Finally, the instructor discusses comments, suggestions, and plans for change with his or her students. SGID has had a number of impacts at Seattle Central Community College, where the technique has been used extensively for years:

> In response to course-specific suggestions, instructors
> have clarified course structure, provided additional
> examples and preexamination reviews, eliminated non-
> productive exercises, and added more challenging home-
> work. Moreover, textbooks have been replaced, testing
> procedures altered, classroom activities redesigned. In
> an unpublished survey of faculty opinion...instructors
> described the wide range of adjustments that 95 percent
> of them had made (W.E. Bennett 1987, p. 103).

Several variations of these interview techniques—hybrids of the group discussion method and SGID—have apparently also proven effective (Heppner and Johnston 1994; Kyger 1984). A quality-control circle, for example, is essentially different from the class interview. The first purpose of a quality-control circle is "to provide a vehicle for regularly collecting thoughtful feedback from students on their assessments of readings, exams, activities, and major assignments" (Cross and Angelo 1988, p. 160). The professor begins by explaining this purpose to the class and asks for volunteers to serve as members of a quality-control circle for the class. The resulting circle is introduced to the entire class, and the rest of the members of the class are encouraged to seek out members of the circle—their representatives for quality control—to provide comments, criticism, or suggestions about the course for discussion with the instructor at regular meetings with the members of the circle. Experience with these circles in history and chemistry classes at Penn State indicates that students "seemed to appreciate especially the idea of a faculty member allowing them to participate in class decisions, listening to their suggestions, and responding to those suggestions" (Kogut 1984, p. 125).

Classroom Assessment

Classroom assessment, another strategy for listening to students, comprises a wide range of methods that college teachers can use to "obtain useful feedback on what, how much, and how well their students are learning[, which they] can then use . . . to refocus their teaching to help students make their learning more efficient and more effective" (Angelo and Cross 1993, p. 3). In every class, there are "gaps" between what a teacher thinks he or she is teaching and what students are actually learning. Classroom assessment helps instructors to monitor students' learning continuously so that they can identify those gaps and change their teaching behaviors appropriately. Informal techniques to obtain information about students' learning can be used well in advance of the points at which formal evaluation procedures (tests, for example) are used to judge learning and assign grades. The focus is sharpened when faculty keep "asking themselves three questions: 'What are the essential skills and knowledge I am trying to teach?' [teaching goals] 'How can I find out whether students are learning them?' [assessment techniques] 'How can I help students learn better?' [informed instructional improvement]. As teachers work closely with students to answer these questions, they improve their teaching skills and gain new insights" (p. 5).

Most faculty start using classroom assessment with some good, simple techniques that are generalizable to almost any class in any field (Angelo and Cross 1993). For example, the "one-minute paper" merely asks students to write a short response to two questions near the end of the class period: (1) "What is the most important thing you learned in class today?" and (2) "What question remains uppermost in your mind?" (Angelo 1991a, p. 9). Another simple technique collects much useful information by asking students to write a brief response to "What was the 'muddiest point' in my lecture today?" (p. 10). An equally generalizable, but slightly more elaborate, starter technique is called "RSQC2," asking students to write brief notes near the end of class in which they recall the key points of the class, summarize those points in a sentence or two, ask questions about those key points, make comments about how they felt during the presentation of the material on those points, and connect the key points to the content covered in the previous class session (Angelo 1990, p. 74). Obtaining midterm or fast feedback about one's teaching is also a form of classroom assessment. An instructor can use many effective ways to target this early-term student feedback or ETSF (Rando and Lenze 1994), including the refreshing approach of asking students at the start of the course, before any teaching takes place, "how they would like to be taught and treated" (Rallis 1994, p. 258). One very productive approach at this point is to ask students on the first day of class to write out their answers to the question, "What are your pet peeves about college instructors?" (p. 258).

Assuming that assessing students' learning is a particularly important part of making informed improvements in instruction, it is useful to think of the several key types of learning one might want to assess. For example, professors might want to make sure they use techniques that assess students' *declarative* learning (the facts and principles of the field), their *procedural* learning (the required skills of the field), their *conditional* learning (when and where to apply the facts, principles, and skills of the field), and their *reflective* learning (self-awareness of interests, attitudes, and values) (Angelo 1991b). Over 60 specific classroom assessment techniques have now been indexed by the name of the technique, the teaching goal being assessed, and the disciplines in which the technique is particularly useful, with a description, purpose, related teaching goals, suggestions for use, discipline-based examples, procedures, suggested data analyses, ideas for adapting, pros, cons, caveats, references, and resources for each technique (Angelo and Cross 1993).

Reports of successful experiences with the use of classroom assessment for improving instruction are now widespread. Many detailed reports have been published, documenting its use and its positive impact on students' learning and on the quality of teaching in a variety of disciplines, including accounting (Angelo and Cross 1993; Cottell 1991; Matoney 1988); anthropology, astronomy, criminal justice, mathematics, nursing, physical education, political science, speech communication, statistics (Angelo and Cross 1993); psychology (Angelo and Cross 1993; Stevenson 1988; Walker 1991); art (Holmes 1988); business (Lord 1988); composition (Kort 1991); education (Brittingham 1988); and physics (Nakaji 1991).

The Student Visitor in the Classroom

Professors' inviting students into their classrooms who are not "official" members of the class but are trained in techniques of classroom observation prompts an especially distinctive way of receiving student feedback. The primary purpose of a student-visitor program "is to provide confidential observations/feedback . . . to enhance an instructor's effectiveness in helping students learn. Listening to this student voice allows faculty members to gain a broader perspective on their teaching *and* their students' learning" (Sorenson 1994, p. 98). Faculty participants in these programs are usually volunteers; they frequently are new and junior faculty, or faculty who are teaching new courses or experimenting with new techniques, or even well-established, excellent teachers who want to get better still.

In the well-known program at St. Olaf College, student visitors are usually recommended by faculty, especially by faculty who previously have used a visitor (Helling and Kuhlmann 1988). The training of student visitors includes developing facility with classroom observation instruments (which could include viewing videotapes of real classes at other institutions); engaging in role playing to learn effective techniques of giving feedback; and learning to describe specific behaviors instead of making general comments (including particular behaviors that a teacher wants to work on as well as behaviors that are already effective) (pp. 106–7). As part of the visitor-training program at Brigham Young University, visitors are required to "perform a practice visit to one of three volunteer 'guinea pig' professors . . . and write up an observation before they receive their first official assignment" (Sorenson 1994, p. 100).

In the program at Brigham Young University, student visitors perform a variety of different roles:

> *(1)* Recorder/Observer. *The student observers record in writing what happened in class, focusing on* how *the class proceeded, not necessarily* what *was taught. . . . (2)* Faux Student. *Here the student observers take notes as though they were actual students enrolled in the class. This role emphasizes recording* what *was taught rather than* how *it was taught. . . . (3)* Filmmaker. *The students film the class and give the video tapes to the instructors. . . . (4)* Interviewer. *In this model, the professors leave class*

15 minutes early, and the student observers talk with the
class members. . . . (5) Primed Student. *Here the profes-*
sors tell the student observers what to look for. . . . (6)
Student Consultant. *This model implies an ongoing series*
of observations and an evolving relationship between the
observed and the observers (Sorenson 1994, pp. 101–2).

The last role in the list hints at one of the major advantages
of a student visitor compared to a colleague observer: A
student visitor can attend class continuously throughout the
semester, unlike a colleague, who might be able to manage
only one or two visits.

The teacher becomes accustomed to the observer's pres-
ence; the observer develops a real sense of what this class
is like from day to day and can distinguish between a
chance occurrence and a consistent practice. As the
semester proceeds, the observer monitors the teacher's
progress in implementing modifications, and the observ-
er's presence keeps the teacher working at it. By the end
of the term, there has been enough practice so that the
desired behavior is likely to continue (Helling and
Kuhlmann 1988, p. 109).

The primary purpose of a student-visitor program "is to provide confidential observations/feedback . . . to enhance an instructor's effectiveness in helping students learn.

So far, no experimental or other "hard" evidence exists of
the impact of student-visitor programs on the improvement
of teaching. What we do have instead are the consistently
positive evaluative responses of faculty participants and
program coordinators. For example:

Speaking about her experience with the Classroom
Student Observer Program, one BYU professor reported,
"It made me more 'self-conscious' in a positive way. It
clearly helped my teaching and made it more responsive
to students' needs.". . . A comment on the timeliness of
the feedback came from a Carleton professor, who said,
"It's a fine sounding board for regular fine-tuning,
which I like to give courses while they are in process, not
just after they are over" (Sorenson 1994, p. 103).

The Teaching Culture, Instructional
Change, and the Voice of Students
As we examine various ways that students can provide infor-

mative feedback, we do not want to forget about potential connections with the elements of a supportive teaching culture and the mechanisms of the process of instructional change (see figure 1 on p. 17). The example started near the end of the last section continues here to show the relevance of certain elements of the teaching culture and to enable discussion of the *changing* stage of the process of improving instruction.

Suppose our professor meets with her department chair to discuss her interests and concerns about how to teach using problem-solving groups. Following her department chair's invitation, she observes her chair using these groups in a class similar to her own, for several consecutive class sessions early in the fall term. Suppose further that she decides to adopt her chair's active learning techniques in her own class. Next, she decides to obtain informative feedback on the effectiveness of this approach, ideas about how to improve her use of it, and insights to help her fine-tune it with a few "innovative" modifications of her own. To find out how well her students are learning and what would help them learn more, she uses several classroom assessment techniques and collects informal early feedback from her students. She also has a student visitor—trained in classroom observation by the staff of the campus teaching center— observe two sessions and provide her with written feedback. Finally, she asks a consultant from the campus teaching center to conduct a small-group instructional diagnosis and provide her with additional feedback and guidance on how to make effective use of problem-solving groups.

In this example, the predominant sources of informative feedback are the students. The mechanisms of the changing stage of instructional change are present. The professor learns and experiments with new behavior in several ways. Initially, she relies on *identification*, when she adopts the chair's problem-solving groups in her own class. Later, she uses *scanning* when she seeks feedback in various forms from her students and guidance from both a student visitor and a teaching consultant. Elements of a supportive teaching culture are also present: a department chair that supports the improvement of instruction and the availability of the resources of a campus teaching center.

COLLEAGUES, CONSULTANTS, AND CHAIRS

Research has shown that important characteristics of a campus culture that supports teaching include opportunities for interaction and collaboration between colleagues regarding teaching (Ferren 1989; LaCelle-Peterson and Finkelstein 1993), campus teaching centers with trained teaching consultants (Aitken and Sorcinelli 1994; Ambrose 1995), and supportive and effective department chairs (Massy, Wilger, and Colbeck 1994; Wright and O'Neil 1994). In a relatively recent survey of faculty developers at 155 colleges and universities, 74 percent of the respondents rated "colleagues as catalysts for evaluating/facilitating teaching" as a current or desired and planned strategy for improving teaching, 82 percent rated "individual consultation" as a current or desired and planned strategy for improving instruction, and 76 percent rated "training department chairs to facilitate teaching" as a current or desired and planned strategy (Kurfiss and Boice 1990, p. 77). This section examines selected strategies for improving instruction based on professors' receiving informative feedback about their teaching from colleagues, consultants, and department chairs.

Traditional, but still effective, practices for encouraging collegial interaction and collaboration on teaching issues have often focused on such activities as faculty seminars (Ambrose 1990), workshops (Eison and Stevens 1995; Paulsen 1992), and colloquia (Ferren 1989). Developments in a variety of areas—for example, action science (Argyris, Putnam, and Smith 1985), reflective practice (Schon 1983, 1987), and adult learning theory (Brookfield 1986; Candy 1991; Merriam 1993)—continue to encourage faculty developers to expand the range of strategies for improving instruction. The next two subsections examine strategies for improving instruction that are consistent with recent advances in adult learning theory related to self-directed learning—colleagues as coaches and colleagues as team teachers.

Colleagues as Coaches

Like all adults, college teachers are capable of self-directed learning, including learning connected with their teaching. Recent conceptualizations of self-directed learning have revealed several key dimensions of the construct (Caffarella 1993; Candy 1991). This discussion focuses on four in particular—personal autonomy, self-management, learner control, and autodidaxy (Candy 1991). An adult learner is considered *autonomous* when he or she conceives of learning goals and plans, exercises free choice in thought and action, rationally evaluates alternative actions, carries plans through to completion, values self-mastery, and has a concept of self as autonomous (pp. 108–9). Adults engage in *self-management* when they have both the "willingness and ability to manage [their] overall learning endeavors" (p. xvii). *Learner control* refers to the extent to which the teacher or learner has "control over valued instructional functions" (p. 11), and *autodidaxy* is the extent to which an adult learner engages in the "independent pursuit of learning without formal institutional support" (p. xvii). "The autodidact[, however,] might make extensive use of a 'guide' or 'helper' (or perhaps more than one) to assist with a range of factors from . . . utilization of specific resources to management of the learning process itself" (p. 16).

Such traditional strategies for the improvement of teaching as workshops, seminars, or professional consultation in effect assume professors are self-directed learners in terms of personal autonomy (they participate voluntarily) and self-management (they are capable of selecting a strategy from available alternatives that will meet their perceived needs for improving instruction). Only a small range of strategies, however, assume professors are self-directed learners in terms of learner control (they can set their own goals for improving teaching, identify appropriate means for achieving those goals, and accurately assess the degree to which they have achieved their goals) or of autodidaxy (they can pursue instructional improvement independently and informally by seeking advice about teaching from colleagues or through informal feedback from other sources). Certain strategies to improve teaching can, however, promote autodidactic self-directed learning among faculty:

> *Some instructional development offices support or "formalize" these activities through "peer consultation programs" or "peer mentoring." When this support includes the provision of resources, materials, and other ways for faculty to gain "expertise," autodidactic self-directed learning may be fostered* (Cranton 1994, p. 733).

When professors interact with their colleagues as coaches (or as team teachers), they are using strategies for improving instruction that engage them as self-directed learners along each of the four designated dimensions. They are personally "autonomous" and exercise free choice in their decision to participate. They are willing and able to initiate, plan, and "manage" a self-chosen educational program about their teaching. They have complete "control" over all decision making with regard to setting goals, selecting means for reaching those goals, and assessing the degree to which the goals are achieved. And they are "autodidactic" because their strategies for improving instruction depend on seeking informal feedback about their teaching from their colleagues.

Before turning to descriptions and analyses of specific activities, programs, and projects of collegial coaching (and their implications for self-directed learning), a word about definitions is in order. It has been argued that "peer" should be reserved for faculty who share the same disciplinary expertise, while "colleague" should refer to faculty who are from other disciplines (Cashin 1989). It has also been pointed out that "colleague" is the more appropriate term for general use because "peer" suggests an equality of status; thus, "colleague" could be used to refer to all faculty, even if they are of different rank or are department chairs (Centra 1993). The two words are used interchangeably here, although appropriate distinctions are made between colleagues who come from the same or different disciplines.

The term "coaching" comes from the process of developing and incorporating new skills into the repertoire of athletes (Joyce and Showers 1982). This process has been found to be analogous to the challenges of transfer of training in teacher education programs. Unlike professors, who receive little if any training in teaching skills in their graduate programs, elementary and secondary teachers typically complete substantial training programs as part of their formal education. Researchers have found that the transfer of teaching skills from the training setting to those needed in the classroom is greatly enhanced through the use of peer coaching. Furthermore, peer coaching has been found to promote the "development of norms of collegiality and experimentation" regarding teaching issues (Showers 1985, p. 45). And coaching has a role in the transfer of training:

Each teacher practiced the teaching strategy . . . and, finally, in teams of two, they began to try it out with the most able students in their elective creative writing classes. One team member taught while the other observed and offered constructive criticism; then they switched places. Sometimes they taught together. Each practiced several times with the "coaching partner" present to reflect on progress and to offer suggestions about how to improve the next trial (Joyce and Showers 1982, p. 4).

This approach has been called "technical coaching" (Kinsella 1995), as it often emphasizes developing skill with a particular teaching technique. "Collegial coaching," on the other hand, "concentrates on the individual areas the observed teacher wishes to improve . . . [and] leads colleagues to reflect together on personally relevant issues of teaching and learning" (p. 116). An eclectic approach to coaching is recommended (Kinsella 1995) so that programs could draw from either model as desired.

Two primary activities are involved in collegial coaching: the observation of classroom teaching and instructional consultation. Most scholars agree that evaluative data based primarily on observation by colleagues in the classroom might not be appropriate for use in personnel decisions regarding promotion and tenure. Their concerns are largely based on several findings of a study of colleagues' ratings of 54 college teachers, based solely on observations in the classroom. These findings include low agreement among colleague raters (low reliability of ratings), very high average ratings given, and low variance in those ratings (Centra 1975). Yet most scholars also agree that observation in the classroom and instructional consultation with colleagues *can* be an effective strategy for improving instruction (Braskamp and Ory 1994; Centra 1993; Cohen and McKeachie 1980; French-Lazovik 1981; Seldin 1988; Weimer 1990).

The consultation component of collegial coaching is hardly limited to just observing and discussing classroom behavior; it can also involve the peer review of course materials (outlines, readings, evaluation procedures, and the like). A recent survey of 331 faculty developers in the United States, Canada, the United Kingdom, and Australasia reveals that respondents rated "consultation on course materials with faculty peers" as one of the top 10 most effective strategies for improving instruction (Wright and O'Neil 1995, pp. 12–13). "As faculty developers, survey respondents know that this activity [of consultation on course materials] is a good way to encourage a collegial approach to teaching improvement" (p. 25). A recent review of the literature on collegial coaching identifies evaluation of course materials as one of the common functions performed for faculty by their coaches (Harcharik 1994), and an extensive review of the literature on collaborative peer review examines this function in detail as one of five "methods that have been used by colleagues to assess their peers' teaching for the purpose of instructional improvement" (Keig and Waggoner 1994, p. 41). Further, faculty developers experienced in the development and use of teaching portfolios recommend that an instructor prepare such a portfolio in collaboration with a colleague, consultant, or department chair (Seldin 1993; Seldin, Annis, and Zubizarreta 1995).

A number of scholars have identified the particular aspects of teaching for which the examination of course material by a collegial coach provides useful feedback (Braskamp, Brandenburg, and Ory 1984; Braskamp and Ory 1994; Cashin 1989; Centra 1993; Centra, Froh, Gray, and Lambert 1987; Cohen and McKeachie 1980; Seldin 1988). The most comprehensive list of teaching competencies is arranged into three categories "according to the medium from which information could be obtained": syllabus; readings and other learning activities; and tests, papers, projects, presentations, and other assigned academic work (Keig and Waggoner 1994, pp. 61–62). An abbreviated but representative list includes course content (Is it consistent with contemporary knowledge of the subject? Are the breadth and depth of coverage appropriate for the course?), course syllabus (Does it adequately outline the sequence of topics to be covered?), course objectives (Do they represent the desired mastery of the subject? Are course objectives clear to the students?), learning approaches (Are the learning approaches—texts, reading lists, films, assignments, lectures, discussions—suitable to course content and objectives? Is the course well paced?), textbooks and handouts (Are they appropriate to the course level? Is the material up to date?), readings (Do they supplement the lecture notes and class discussion?), assignments (Do the assignments reflect course objectives?), examinations and grading (Is the content of exams representative of the course content and objectives?

Are exam items clear and well written? Is the distribution of grades appropriate to the level of the course and preparation of the students enrolled?) (Seldin 1988, p. 51).* Many of the features of teaching included in teaching portfolios to be reviewed by peers (work samples and reflections on those samples) overlap with the course materials included on this list and are already typically included in faculty reviews of teaching (see, e.g., Seldin 1993, pp. 77–78).

Collegial coaching (observation and consultation) projects have been undertaken at a variety of colleges and universities, including University of Cincinnati (Sweeney and Grasha 1979), Texas Tech University (Skoog 1980), University of Maine at Farmington (Ferren and Geller 1983), University of Kentucky Community College System (Kerwin 1985; Kerwin and Rhoads 1993), Indiana University (Barnett 1983), University of South Carolina (Bell, Dobson, and Gram 1977), University of Maryland University College (Millis 1989, 1992; Millis and Kaplan 1995), California State Polytechnic University (Harcharik 1994), New Jersey Institute for Collegiate Teaching and Learning (Golin 1990; Katz and Henry 1988; Smith and LaCelle-Peterson 1991), Oklahoma Junior College (Minor and Preston 1991), Ball State University (Annis 1989), New York University (Rorschach and Whitney 1986), State University of New York at Cortland (Shatzky and Silberman 1986), and University of Chicago (Tobias 1986). These programs generally have in common all or most of the following seven features: (1) an underlying philosophy, (2) a procedure for selecting participants, (3) a training program for collegial coaches (observer/consultants), (4) a preobservation conference, (5) one or more classroom visits and observations, (6) a postobservation conference, and (7) an evaluation of effectiveness by participants. Each aspect is discussed in the following paragraphs.

An underlying philosophy

The New Jersey Master Faculty Program has a particularly well-reasoned underlying philosophy regarding what makes it work. The ideas used to explain why this particular collegial coaching program is so effective connect well with (1)

---

*A useful set of sample questions covering the items on this list, as well as a sample form for use in the process of collegial review of course materials, is available in Ory (1989, pp. 64–65).

the principal features of the general model of instructional improvement delineated earlier in this report—unfreezing (disconfirmation, comparison, and safety), changing (cognitive redefinition through scanning or identification), and refreezing (sustaining change through integration and reconfirmation; (2) some of the key characteristics of a supportive teaching culture identified earlier—for example, the importance of opportunities for interaction and collaboration among faculty and a sense of faculty "ownership" of the process of instructional improvement; (3) the concepts of reflective practice, action science, and transformative learning, which frame the analysis of the teacher as reflective practitioner; and (4) the dimensions of self-directedness in the adult learner (autonomy, self-management, learner control, and autodidaxy).

It works because the process is . . . Ongoing. *Faculty who return from one-shot development experiences, such as conferences or workshops, return to an unchanged environment. Soon their energy dissipates, the new ideas fade. But faculty who observe and are observed, who interview students, who meet with a partner, are engaged in an ongoing process. The classroom is not the same. There's someone new in it, someone on our side. Within the peer relationship we feel safe; we receive the support we need in order to run risks. Feedback from students and our partner is continuous. In response, we try some new things, and we get feedback on them. . . .* Decentralized. *The faculty pair is largely autonomous. It charts its own directions. . . . Meeting regularly, . . . the pair shapes its own version of the process. . . .* Faculty-owned. *Very quickly faculty claim ownership. We see that unlike much faculty development, the peer collaboration and interviewing belong to us. . . . Faculty respond with real creativity and initiative to a program that they perceive as not only for them but by them. . . .* Transforming. *. . . Collaborating with a peer is itself transforming. We see that our frustrations and hopes are not unique. The isolation of teaching is subverted. Regardless of what else we learn, we learn how much we need one another. . . . The new relationship with students whom we interview, like the relationship with our partner, transforms*

*our attitude toward teaching and learning . . . [and in
the words of a program participant,] "Both observing
and being observed have caused me to look very critically at my own teaching; I have become acutely aware
of what I do in my classes"* (Golin 1990, pp. 9–10).

A procedure for selecting participants

Participants in most collegial coaching programs are volunteers, and they usually work in pairs. Sometimes the collegial pairs are from the same or a related field; other times
they are from very different fields. When the targets of
observation and consultation are content-related course
materials or aspects of teaching related to knowledge of
pedagogical content (Shulman 1986, 1987, 1989), a
colleague from the same field is especially helpful. But
when the purpose of observation and consultation is related
to improving *general* (rather than *content-specific*) teaching
skills, collegial feedback and discussion could focus too
much on specific content and thus interfere with the necessary attention to behaviors targeted for observation and
improvement (Keig and Waggoner 1994; Menges 1987;
Weimer 1990), and in this case, a colleague outside one's
field could prove more helpful. Ultimately, the choice
depends upon the purpose of the collegial coaching project.

A training program for collegial coaches

Most training programs for collegial coaches focus on developing their skills in observation and in giving feedback during consultation. The University of Maine at Farmington
brought in an outside consultant to conduct two half-day
training sessions. The relatively thorough training program
contains a very important component:

> *The second half-day session concentrated on alterna-
> tive observation approaches, techniques for recording
> data, and analysis of data to prepare for a conference.
> The two-person teams then visited a regular class in
> session to practice the classroom consultant process.
> Following the class visit, the workshop participants
> returned to share their experiences, analyze their data,
> discuss effective ways of giving feedback, and plan for
> their work together during the rest of the semester*
> (Ferren and Geller 1983, p. 84).

The Teaching Consultation Program for the University of Kentucky Community College System adds a special "teaching consultants workshop" to the typical training program for collegial coaches. An important part of the training program takes place six weeks into the semester after all faculty consultants have both observed and videotaped their colleagues. At this point, all faculty consultants participate in a special two-day workshop. Each collegial consultant (coach) makes a 25-minute presentation to all the other participants. Consultants in turn present short oral descriptions of the colleague they are coaching, then show a 10-minute videotape that illustrates the colleague's teaching in the classroom. At that point, all participants join in a group analysis and discussion of the teaching behaviors of each colleague and jointly explore strategies for improvement (Kerwin and Rhoads 1993, p. 72).

The overall process of consultation in most collegial coaching projects clearly follows three phases of instructional observation and diagnosis.

A preobservation conference

The overall process of consultation in most collegial coaching projects clearly follows three phases of instructional observation and diagnosis (first described by Bergquist and Phillips 1975, pp. 88–90). The first phase is customarily a preobservation conference between the coach and the teacher to be observed. During this conference, participants share teaching goals (and sometimes course materials) and identify specific behaviors about which the teacher wants feedback (Millis 1989; Sweeney and Grasha 1979). The coach and teacher also agree on the observation techniques and instruments to be used in the next phase of the process. These agreements constitute a sort of contract, and although "the contract is not restrictive, it does assure that the observation and feedback will be directed toward the observer's concerns" (Skoog 1980, p. 23).

Classroom visits and observations

The second phase is the observation itself. It is often carried out by the coach's use of an agreed-upon observation instrument. For example, observations might be guided by a detailed checklist of specific behaviors, such as a guide for observation that contains nearly 300 specific behaviors arranged into three major categories (teaching through presentation, teaching through involvement, and teaching through questioning) (Helling 1988, pp. 150–54). Sometimes observation is based on a more condensed narrative form that poses general questions about various aspects of teaching that the coach answers with written comments (Millis and Kaplan 1995, p. 148). Some recommend a more detailed narrative form (see, e.g., Sorcinelli 1984) that provides sets of questions to be addressed during the preobservation conference, the classroom observation, and the postobservation conference (Keig and Waggoner 1994, pp. 45–49).

Each of these approaches to classroom observation is customarily used when the perspective of the visitor is that of the faculty observer—a nonparticipant in classroom activities. An entirely different approach to classroom observation in collegial coaching projects is the use of an observer who is a full participant in classroom activities (see, e.g., Annis 1989; Rorschach and Whitney 1986; Shatzky and Silberman 1986; Tobias 1986, 1988). In such cases, observation is, as much as possible, from the student's perspective, with the observations still shared between experienced professors. In most such projects, collegial coaching pairs remain participant observers in each other's classes over the course of an entire semester. A professor of English and a professor of chemistry at the State University of New York at Cortland elaborate on the rationale for this approach:

> *Where this endeavor differs from other techniques, including team teaching, is that the instructors involved are ideally from completely different disciplines. This is so that little, if any, of their background gives them an advantage over the other students in understanding the material. In other words, when the instructor attends a colleague's class, it is as complete a learning experience as can possibly be simulated. . . . As master-students, we were able to talk to our fellow students and find out more about their understanding of the material and the teaching methods than we could as faculty. (We were, after all, in the same boat [as] they were.) Moreover, because neither of us had any prior knowledge of the material covered, it was easier to understand and empathize with those students having difficulty. But it was also true that we could better evaluate the rigor of the courses we taught and judge whether or not students were being conscientious in*

*their efforts to learn the material and do the course
work* (Shatzky and Silberman 1986, pp. 119–20).

A postobservation conference
During the third phase, the postobservation conference, the
coach presents feedback regarding the specific behaviors the
teacher targeted in an objective and descriptive (rather than
judgmental) manner, and encourages the teacher to develop
strategies for change based on the feedback provided. It is
the coach's responsibility to allow the teacher to make all
change-related choices, resisting the temptation to shape or
make those choices *for* the colleague (Millis 1992). "To avoid
a prescriptive stance, rather than offer direct advice, [coach-
es] must encourage colleagues or peers to explore teaching
options, starting with some that have been suggested in the
[feedback]. . . . The instructor makes choices about areas to
change to enhance the teaching and specific strategies to
assist in making those changes" (p. 198).

An evaluation of effectiveness by participants
The final aspect of good practice in collegial coaching is the
need for a session between coach and teacher near the end
of the process that centers on the assessment of effectiveness, focusing on "such things as how successful they felt,
how helpful they were to the teacher, and whether or not
any interpersonal or other barriers existed while working
together" (Sweeney and Grasha 1979, p. 55). A particularly
creative (if not courageous) variation on collegial coaching
was carried out recently at the University of New Orleans
(Bogotch and Bernard 1994). At least two aspects of this
project are noteworthy exceptions to the norms that have
arisen for collegial coaching. First, the coach was a doctoral
student of the professor seeking feedback—more appropriate than it might appear at first blush because the student
was an expert in coaching and a central administrator in the
public schools, while the courses the professor taught were
in the field of educational administration: "We deliberately
sought to turn a traditional professor–graduate student relationship on its head, consequently identifying the graduate
student *cum* expert in coaching and the professor *cum*
teacher-learner" (p. 2). Second, although the coach was
present in the classroom for every class, she was neither an

official student in the class nor a participant observer. The project resulted in numerous constructive changes in the teacher's behavior, particularly in the teacher's encouragement of students' participation and effective use of small-group activities.

While "authors of programs . . . report that faculty members believed their teaching had improved as a result of feedback provided by colleagues," evaluation of programs appears to be somewhat limited (Keig and Waggoner 1994, p. 95). At least one recent exception to the lack of evaluation is noteworthy, however. In an experimental design to assess the effectiveness of the Teaching Consultation Program at the University of Kentucky Community College System, members of the experimental group worked with faculty consultants (coaches), who directly observed them and videotaped them in their classrooms in an effort to develop goals for improving teaching and strategies to achieve the goals (Rozeman and Kerwin 1991). Experimental and control groups were compared in terms of changes in their student ratings of teaching between end-of-semester assessments before and after the intervention. Results "indicated that for 'Overall rating of the teacher's ability to teach,' the experimental group made significantly positive improvements on the [ratings] instrument as compared to the control group. . . . These improvements persisted through to the third administration . . . one year after the initial testing and one semester after the intervention" (pp. 227–28). Additional studies like this one are needed to provide more substantial evidence to supplement the self-reports of participants and program coordinators regarding the effectiveness of collegial coaching as a strategy for improving instruction.

Colleagues as Team Teachers

A recent qualitative investigation of the sources of intrinsic rewards in college teaching involved individual interviews with 52 faculty at six large research universities, as well as interviews with an additional 36 faculty from two of the institutions. While teaching has many intrinsic rewards, faculty need to be reminded of them through opportunities to talk about their teaching with their colleagues (Froh, Menges, and Walker 1993, p. 93). Interviews with 111 senior faculty at 11 colleges and universities revealed that one of the most potent sources of faculty development and vitality in teaching comes from opportunities to interact and collaborate with colleagues within the context of "team teaching," which faculty report as "their most meaningful teaching interactions" (LaCelle-Peterson and Finkelstein 1993, p. 28). Nursing faculty reported considerable interaction through team teaching individual courses, suggesting that as a result of these and other teaching-related interactions, teaching had clearly improved in areas where colleagues in other departments were still struggling. Faculty in the laboratory sciences reported that their "most significant interaction with colleagues and students took place in laboratory settings," where discussions about teaching were encouraged by the sharing of space and equipment in the laboratory (p. 28). Faculty also described significant collegial interactions about teaching associated with the grading of writing assignments or common examinations within the context of departmental courses with multiple sections.

A relatively recent review of the literature on faculty collaboration through team teaching revealed three primary benefits for professors—the "development of their teaching ability, new intellectual stimulation, and a closer connection to the university or college as a community" (Austin and Baldwin 1991, p. 41). The capacity of team teaching to improve instruction apparently derives from the opportunities for interaction provided by collaboration in teaching, through which colleagues come to trust one another, observe each other teach, and discuss their ideas and concerns about teaching (pp. 41–42).

Team teaching can be defined as "two or more trainers or teachers collaborating over the design or implementation of the same course" (Easterby-Smith and Olve 1984, p. 221). Team teaching is not a new concept, having been used widely in elementary and secondary schools since the 1950s and expanded greatly in colleges and universities during the 1960s as part of the movement toward student-centered learning (Easterby-Smith and Olve 1984; Heath, Carlson, and Kurtz 1987). Five different models of team teaching have been developed, distinguished by the roles played by team members in the design and implementation of teams (Easterby-Smith and Olve 1984). During the design phase, planning is usually primarily under the control of one member (solo design) or performed collaboratively with all team members contributing (joint design). During implementation, the roles of team members can be divided according to the content specialty of each member (content implementation) or the component activities of teaching—lecturing, discussion, grading, and so on (process implementation). In some cases, team members jointly plan or design the class but without clear divisions between the roles of members during implementation.

The five models of team teaching can be arranged from the least collaborative to the most collaborative (Easterby-Smith and Olve 1984). A *star team* is one in which one teacher is totally in charge of designing or planning the course, while guest lecturers or "visiting stars" are invited to the classroom during implementation to address their different content specialties in ways that fit the primary teacher's course design. Guest lecturers are present at different times and do not collaborate or interact with one another. A *hierarchical team* also has one teacher who is primarily in charge of the design of the course, but during implementation, the roles of other team members are divided according to different aspects of teaching, with each team member responsible for a specific aspect (for example, the central teacher handles the lectures, while other members conduct supplemental discussions). This model describes well the features of a typical team comprising a professor and several teaching assistants in many universities. But because of the usual absence of meaningful interaction among team members in these two least collaborative models, whether or not teaching improves remains an unanswered question.

Each member of a *specialist team* contributes to the design and planning of the course, according to his or her content specialties. During implementation, lecturers' roles are also divided according to their content specialties. Because more than one team member customarily is present at every class session, team members can learn from each other in terms of both content and teaching methods. Three professors at the New England College of Optometry, for example, report on a successful team teaching experience consistent with the characteristics of the specialist team model (Heath, Carlson, and Kurtz 1987). Participants report that under the conditions of this approach, team "members can learn new teaching techniques from one another and receive continual peer evaluation at the same time" (p. 77). Unlike the star and hierarchical models, the specialist model offers a variety of opportunities for collegial discussion about teaching issues.

The members of a *generalist team* have similar content backgrounds and share joint responsibility for all aspects of designing the course. During implementation, the roles of different members are divided by time or according to the different aspects of instruction for which they are responsible (for example, introduction, conceptual presentation, class exercises, and so on).

An *interactive team* is the most collaborative of all team teaching models. Such teams usually include only two members, who fully share every aspect of the design and planning of their course. In-class roles are often not fully planned in advance, and contributions from students or a participating team member can influence both the content and teaching methods that emerge during implementation. Members of an interactive team "literally co-teach by jointly discussing with each other and the students the day's topic" (Austin and Baldwin 1991, p. 37). Some scholars argue that this interactive model is the only one that represents true team teaching and is the type of collaboration in teaching that most likely leads to improvements in instruction (Quinn and Kanter 1984; Weimer 1990): "When faculty truly share the responsibility for a course, few report participating in the experience without its having significant effects on their instruction" (Weimer 1990, p. 128).

Several teams have published reports of successful experiences with the interactive model of team teaching (see, e.g., French and Sands 1993; Fuchs and Moore 1988; Tannahill and Robertson 1986). At the University of Colorado at Denver, for example, one experience with team teaching was a combination of "co-teaching" and "peer coaching" (French and Sands 1993). The teachers jointly designed their course and implemented that design by sharing responsibilities for teaching, advising, and grading. Both were present at every class, co-teaching by alternating "lead" and "support" positions during each class session. The "support role" included facilitating discussion, monitoring and recording teachers' and students' actions, and providing additional examples to clarify key points. The two-person team held three-hour meetings each week to review the previous class and to plan the next. Both professors experienced tension regarding control over the organization and coverage of content, and they found the experience to be very time-consuming, especially because of the need to make all decisions by consensus. Peer coaching involved giving each other regular feedback and (collegial) support. One of the primary benefits of co-teaching was their "personal development of teaching skills. By using peer coaching in a course that [they] had cooperatively planned and implemented, receiving feedback felt safe and nonthreatening" (p. 52).

An unusual, but apparently very effective, application of the interactive teaching model was carried out by a professor of teacher education and a junior high school teacher who team taught a fourth grade language arts class (Fuchs and Moore 1988). The college professor and the school teacher planned all classroom activities jointly, taught together in the classroom as a true team, and shared and reflected upon their reactions to the class sessions. The professor had to adapt to feeling like a novice teacher again as well as to the presence of another teacher in the classroom while trying to test out the theories of learning he taught in his teacher education classes. While the professor was experimenting with the role of lead teacher, the school teacher experienced discomfort at having the smooth operation of her classroom disrupted and interjected her own comments to clarify ideas for the students. Both were pleased to see experiments with "wait time" in questioning and the principles of "cooperative learning" actually work in the classroom. They also reported clear benefits from team teaching. For the professor, the examples "used to illustrate a point in college classes [were] more current and relevant." For the school teacher, the instruments used "to measure teacher behaviors and the supportive evaluation of her teaching by the professor . . . increased her teaching effectiveness" (p. 412).

It has been suggested that six types of team members make a winning team: someone dependable, someone inventive, someone brilliant, someone kind, someone who understands compromise, and someone who can create coherence (Rinn and Weir 1984, p. 10). And "anyone considering joint teaching with colleagues" should carefully consider the following recommendations, based on a recent review of the literature on collaborative teaching arrangements:

1. Know your potential collaborators well;
2. Clarify what each person brings to the collaborative relationship;
3. Work out the details in advance;
4. Solicit feedback from students;
5. Renegotiate roles and responsibilities periodically;
6. Cultivate a spirit of camaraderie;
7. Communicate to others the nature of the collaborative arrangement; and
8. If a junior faculty member, be cautious about collaborative teaching, making sure to find out just how team teaching will be viewed, evaluated, and rewarded by the department, college, and university (Baldwin and Austin 1995, pp. 211–13).

Models of Instructional Consultation

One of the most robust empirical findings regarding the effectiveness of various strategies for improving instruction is that consultative sessions about the informative feedback a teacher has received about his or her teaching is consistently associated with more positive future evaluation of the teacher's instruction (Cohen 1980; Levinson-Rose and Menges 1981; L'Hommedieu, Menges, and Brinko 1990; Marsh and Roche 1993; Menges and Brinko 1986). In a recent survey of 331 faculty developers, respondents were asked to rate the potential of various strategies to improve instruction (Wright and O'Neil 1995). The results indicate support for the effectiveness of instructional consultation. Respondents ranked the "availability of expert consultation services regarding such areas as course planning, test construction, and teaching skills" 14th out of 36 strategies, revealing confidence in its potential for promoting the improvement of instruction (p. 36). Moreover, "videotaping classroom teaching for analysis and improvement (often including consultation with a teaching expert)" was ranked 16th overall but 12th out of 36 by faculty developers in the United States and Canada. These results reveal "a fairly high degree of confidence" in the capacity of instructional consultation to improve instruction (p. 25).

A comprehensive process of instructional consultation
Many of the informal processes of consultation carried out in

collegial coaching projects have been formalized in a comprehensive set of routine services provided by the trained consultants who constitute the staff of campus teaching centers. Many consultants at campus teaching centers are former full-time faculty who have been trained and have become highly experienced in instructional consultation. The structure and process of instructional consultation performed by the staff of teaching centers is usually based on the comprehensive model of individual consultation first developed in the early 1970s as part of the Clinic to Improve University Teaching at the University of Massachusetts (Bergquist and Phillips 1977; Povlacs 1988). The model included four basic stages: data collection, data analysis, improvement strategies, and evaluation (Bergquist and Phillips 1977, p. 69).

During *data collection,* the consultant interviews the instructor to obtain information about his or her course objectives, methods, materials, and any particular concerns the instructor might have about his or her teaching; asks the instructor to complete a self-assessment of teaching, using a form with items similar to the ones students will use to rate teaching; observes and videotapes the instructor during classroom teaching; and collects students' ratings of the instructor's teaching. When appropriate, the consultant might collect data from interviews with students and ask peers to observe content-specific aspects of their colleague's teaching in the classroom. During *data analysis and review,* both the instructor and the consultant examine the data from all sources. The instructor identifies specific aspects of teaching that he or she would like to discuss and reaches agreement with the consultant on relative strengths and weaknesses, based on the perceptions of the instructor, the students, and the consultant. During preparation of an *improvement strategy,* the instructor and the consultant describe a significant teaching problem suggested by the data, negotiate objectives for change, and agree on strategies for improvement that could involve changing existing teaching materials or methods, trying a new teaching technique, or engaging in some training. *Evaluation* usually includes additional observation, videotaping, or student ratings (Bergquist and Phillips 1977, pp. 69–78).

A well-known experimental investigation of the effect of this comprehensive model of instructional consultation on improving instruction was conducted in the late 1970s (Erickson and Erickson 1979). The faculty in the experimental group went through all the stages of the procedure described in the preceding paragraph, including examination of data (from self-assessment, student ratings, observation, and videotaping of teaching) and an interview with a consultant, all of which "were used to identify the targets of teaching improvement efforts for each experimental group instructor" (p. 676). Based on ratings late in the semester, "students of experimental group instructors perceived more positive change in teaching performance over the semester than did students of control group instructors" (p. 677). Improved effectiveness was greatest for those skills that had been identified as the targets for improved teaching. Moreover, follow-up student ratings from one to four semesters later showed persistent improvement in teaching over time. A recent well-designed experimental study of the effects of instructional consultation on the improvement of instruction used a consultation process (devised by Wilson [1986]) that was still similar in many respects to the model outlined above, with the notable exception that no observation or videotaping of teaching occurred (Marsh and Roche 1993). Comparing results for the experimental and control groups, the researchers found that the effect of consultation was "stronger for the initially least effective teachers, that improvement [was] largest for the specific areas each teacher targeted as the focus of the intervention," and that the effects of consultation based on "end-of-term feedback [were] stronger than those based on midterm ratings" (p. 247).

Comparing results for the experimental and control groups, the researchers found that the effect of consultation was "stronger for the initially least effective teachers.

The obvious question to ask at this point is "What is it about instructional consultation that promotes instructional improvement?" Notable speculations abound about the answer to this important question. For example, it has been suggested that the positive effects of instructional consultation "occur merely because consultation insures that feedback is actively attended to and processed" (Menges and Brinko 1986, p. 11). Instructional consultation could also be effective because feedback from the consultant helps the instructor translate various perceptions and assessments of teaching (for example, student ratings) into specific teaching behaviors that can be concretely described and easily understood, thereby providing a foundation for change (Murray

1987a, p. 89). It could well be that "a consultant can provide . . . suggestions about alternative methods of teaching"
(McKeachie 1987, p. 6) that constitute the kind of feedback
that helps "teachers know how to make changes" (Centra
1993, p. 84). Expert consultation has also been described as
"the most individualized and context-specific approach to
improvement of classroom teaching" (Tiberius 1995, p. 192).
Others have emphasized the importance of the personal
contact between the consultant and instructor. For example,
when giving feedback, "the consultant develops interpersonal communication with the instructor and uses support
and encouragement to help him or her improve (Gil 1987,
p. 59). And it is also possible that "interpersonal expectations established in the consultation sessions create for some
faculty a desire to fulfill an implied contract with their consultant" (Wilson 1986, p. 211).

In combination, these speculations suggest that consultation can improve teaching through various interpersonal
roles assumed by consultants and effective practices in giving *feedback*. Learning more about the various interpersonal
roles that consultants can assume and about how they can
use effective practices in giving feedback could improve the
effectiveness of a wide range of both formal and informal
processes of instructional consultation. Understanding the
roles of instructional consultants and how to give feedback
effectively could be useful in training faculty to be consultants to their close colleagues or to serve as a consultant on
the staff of the campus teaching center (see Brinko and
Menges *In press* for a useful resource in this area).

The roles of instructional consultants
Much of what we have learned about the practice of instructional consultation has been drawn from the extensive experience of faculty developers rather than from experimental
investigation of the process. Instructional consultation has
been defined as "looking at, interpreting, and analyzing the
individual teacher-client's unique teaching behaviors in a
collaborative, investigative fashion" (Weimer and Lenze
1991, p. 306); the essential purpose or "task of the consultant is to help the client (faculty member) think about what
is happening in his or her teaching and develop some alter-
nate strategies for dealing with the problems" (Lewis 1988,
p. 21). The underlying theory is that "feedback on behavior,

accompanied by support, produces change in behavior" (Povlacs 1988, p. 82).

The consultant assumes a variety of roles during the process of consultation, and they can be arranged according to the phases of the process of instructional consultation (Lewis 1988). For example, during the earliest phases of the process, a consultant is a *data collector* who interviews the instructor about his or her course, attitudes about teaching, self-assessment of teaching, specific concerns about teaching, and personal problems; examines course materials; collects student ratings and interview data; and observes and videotapes actual teaching. During the next phase, the consultant assumes the role of *data manager,* arranging all of the data collected so that it is in an accessible and understandable form for the instructor and is related to the instructor's specific concerns about his or her teaching. The consultant becomes a *facilitator* when the instructor and consultant jointly discuss and interpret the data, explore alternative approaches to teaching, and decide what needs to be done to improve the instructor's teaching. When the instructor begins to experiment with new techniques, the consultant often serves as a *support system* to assist the instructor in the analysis and interpretation of whatever happens during experimentation. If the instructor has personal problems that affect his or her teaching, the consultant (depending on his or her training) might serve as *counselor* or refer the instructor to someone more qualified to perform that role. Finally, as the instructor experiments with new techniques of teaching, the consultant serves as an *information source,* recommending and discussing various available materials on the new technique (pp. 21–26).

During data analysis and review—that is, when the consultant is giving feedback—the role of the consultant becomes "especially complex as it is comprised of those of a colleague, an active listener, [and] a facilitator" (Povlacs 1988, p. 83). When the consultant assumes the role of *colleague,* he or she is perceived by the instructor to be of equal status—that is, someone with college teaching experience as well as experience in the improvement of teaching. Both consultant and instructor view the process as collaborative, not remedial. They analyze the data and make decisions jointly. The consultant is not viewed as an expert; instead, he or she is viewed as one who offers informed guidance. In the role of *active listener,* the consultant relies on skills, such as acceptance of feelings, empathy, probing, paraphrasing, refocusing, and summarizing (pp. 86–91).

Models of consultative interaction

Two separate reviews of the literature have identified at least four basic approaches to (or styles of) consultation. The first identifies four styles called expert, problem-solver, collaborator, and counselor (Dalgaard, Simpson, and Carrier 1982). These styles are similar in many respects to four of the five models identified in the second—product, prescription, collaborative/process, affiliative (Brinko 1990), and confrontational (Brinko 1991). The names of these styles in the first review (Dalgaard, Simpson, and Carrier 1982) emphasize the primary roles the consultant might assume throughout his or her interaction with an instructor. The names given in the second review (Brinko 1990, 1991) are more descriptive of the focus of the relationship and nature of the interaction between consultant and instructor.

In the *product model,* the instructor identifies the problem and its probable solution and then draws upon the expertise of the consultant "to produce a test, slide show, video, lab manual, or other product that can remediate the problem" (Brinko 1991, p. 42). In the *prescription model,* the relationship between consultant and instructor is like the traditional doctor-patient relationship—"the consultant assumes authority and responsibility for identifying, diagnosing, and solving problems" (pp. 43–45). In the *collaborative/process model,* consultants are viewed as collegial facilitators of improvement, while instructors bring their expertise on content to bear on the problem. The instructor and consultant work together to "identify, diagnose, and suggest solutions to problems" (p. 45). Sometimes consultants use the *affiliative model* in which they become counselors, helping the instructor to solve "personal problems that may cause or exacerbate . . . instructional problems" (p. 45). Occasionally, consultants adopt a *confrontational model* to challenge the assumptions of a recalcitrant instructor who may be "denying the problem or is personally or professionally threatened by it" (p. 45).

In an empirical investigation of the interactions of instructional consultation, the verbal behaviors of consultants and instructors engaged in consultation were coded from 10 videotapes of sessions conducted by faculty developers at eight different universities (Brinko 1990). In each case, the consultant provided feedback for the instructor based on classroom observation, videotapes, student ratings, or interviews with students. Each consultant was classified according to which of four models of consultative interaction he or she primarily employed—product, prescriptive, collaborative/process, or affiliative. Among the consultants observed, none used the product or affiliative models, while all of them employed behaviors that fit both the prescriptive and collaborative/process models. And no apparent differences were revealed between novice and experienced consultants. As a group, consultants were more or less evenly distributed across a prescriptive-collaborative continuum; however, six of the 10 were in the moderately to very collaborative range, while only four were in the moderately to very prescriptive range (p. 74). Some faculty developers and other scholars prefer the collaborative/process model as the approach most likely to improve instruction (Braskamp and Ory 1994; Carroll and Goldberg 1989; Cooper 1982; Dalgaard, Simpson, and Carrier 1982; Geis 1991; Povlacs 1988). Others believe that a more flexible approach is necessary because the appropriate model depends on, and will emerge within, the dynamics of each consultative situation (Brinko 1991); moreover, some instructors might not prefer, need, or be ready for the collaborative/process model, which requires a great commitment on the part of both consultant and instructor to be effective (Cash and Minter 1979).

Effective practices for giving feedback

Instructional feedback has been defined as "information provided to instructors about their performance that includes recommendations for future improvement" (Gil 1987, p. 58). This definition of feedback is remarkably similar to the profile of the data review and analysis phase of consultation portrayed in earlier parts of this section. This particular phase of a consultation occurs when the consultant's role becomes the most complex, for the consultant assumes the overlapping roles of colleague, active listener, and facilitator (Povlacs 1988, p. 83). Each aspect of this complex role is associated with the practice of giving feedback to the instructor—the kind of feedback that comprises both information and guidance (that is, suggestions for improvement). The point at which the consultant gives feedback to the instructor, consisting of various types of information about his or her teaching drawn from various sources, has been described as "the moment of truth"; how, then, does one seize the moment? (Geis 1991, p. 7).

A review of the literature on effective practices for giving feedback in the fields of education, psychology, and organizational behavior generated a comprehensive set of 35 specific recommendations that can guide colleagues as coaches and expert consultants toward giving effective feedback to instructors (Brinko 1993). The review provides recommendations on what, when, and how feedback should be given from the perspective of both giver and recipient.

For the giver, feedback is more effective when:

1. Information is gathered from a number of sources;
2. Information is gathered from oneself as well as from others;
3. The source of the information is perceived as credible, knowledgeable, and well-intentioned;
4. The source of feedback is lower or equal in status to the recipient;
5. The information is mediated by a consultant; and
6. The consultant is authentic, respectful, supportive, empathic, nonjudgmental, and able to keep consultations confidential (Brinko 1993, pp. 577–78).

No one mode of giving feedback is most effective, and a variety of modes is best. With regard to content, feedback is more effective when:

1. It contains accurate data and irrefutable evidence;
2. It contains concrete information;
3. It contains specific data;
4. It is focused;
5. It focuses on behavior;
6. It is descriptive;
7. It creates cognitive dissonance; and
8. It contains models for appropriate behavior (Brinko 1993, pp. 579–80).

From the giver's perspective, feedback is more effective when it is given as soon as possible after the performance and is considered a process (pp. 80–81).

Additional recommendations for the effective practice of giving feedback focus on the recipient. In general, feedback is more effective when:

1. Recipients voluntarily engage in the process of feedback;
2. Recipients engage in the process as part of routine professional expectations; and
3. Recipients' amount of experience and developmental stage are considered.

Giving feedback is more effective when the recipient selects the mode of its conveyance (pp. 581–82). The content of feedback is more effective for the recipient when:

1. It is sensitive to the recipient's locus of control;
2. It is sensitive to the recipient's self-esteem;
3. It contains a moderate amount of positive feedback with a selected and limited amount of negative feedback;
4. Its negative information is "sandwiched" between positive information;
5. Its negative information is self-referenced;
6. Its positive information is attributed to internal causes;
7. It creates a moderate amount of cognitive dissonance;
8. It reduces uncertainty for the recipient;
9. It is relevant and meaningful to the recipient;
10. It allows for response and interaction; and
11. It relates to goals that are defined by the recipient or to rewards that result from positive performance (pp. 583–85).

And feedback is more effective for the recipient when it is given frequently but not excessively (p. 585).

Videotapes and consultation
A number of studies have shown that improved instruction is associated considerably with opportunities for instructors to view videotapes of their own (or a colleague's) teaching or to view a model videotape demonstrating effective teaching skills, both with and without consultation (Abbott, Wulff,

and Szego 1989; Boice 1984; Dalgaard 1982; Hendricson, Hawkins, Littlefield, Kleffner, Hudepohl, and Herbert 1983; Levinson-Rose and Menges 1981; McDaniel 1987; Sharp 1981; Taylor-Way 1988; Taylor-Way and Brinko 1989). In an examination of the effects (on subsequent effectiveness in teaching) of viewing oneself on videotape, 22 teaching assistants were assigned to experimental and control groups using a stratified random sampling method. Early in the term, all instructors' classes were videotaped. Next, members of the experimental group attended teaching seminars and had a consultative session with the seminar instructor to view their videotapes, evaluate themselves, and set goals for improving teaching. Late in the semester, all instructors were videotaped again. Trained raters scored the first and second videotapes for each instructor. The experimental group, after the consultation and attending seminars, had significantly higher final ratings than the instructors in the control group (Dalgaard 1982).

In a vivid test of the effects of viewing a demonstration videotape on improving instruction, 37 teaching assistants were assigned randomly to experimental and control groups. Before the semester, all instructors were videotaped teaching a 10-minute lesson. All instructors then attended a seminar on lecturing skills (in two groups), during which members of the experimental group viewed a model videotape on lecturing. All instructors were videotaped teaching another 10-minute lesson during the first week of the semester. Trained raters evaluated both videotapes, and the results indicated that "viewing a model videotape did influence subjects'" teaching positively (Sharp 1981, p. 498).

In another study, faculty observed both themselves and their colleagues on videotape (McDaniel 1987). Members of a faculty seminar on teaching worked toward gaining consensus on what behaviors constitute good teaching. All subjects were videotaped for one hour of teaching, after which they viewed and discussed the videotape with a consultant in terms of their own standards of good teaching and identified specific teaching behaviors to incorporate into their teaching. Later, each instructor was videotaped again, and episodes of effective teaching were extracted from participants' tapes; all faculty in the seminar viewed them together. Many of the faculty found "observing others on videotape to be as beneficial as watching themselves" (p. 99).

A particular advantage of videotaping is that such recordings "can serve wherever and whenever there is a need for instant, accurate, reliable audiovisual feedback that could repeatedly be played back for closer examination and analysis" (Perlberg 1983, p. 634). Videotapes are an external source of information about one's teaching that can promote the process of self-confrontation (Fuller and Manning 1973). One of the primary sources of motivation to change in reviewing videotapes is the instructor's identification of and desire to reduce discrepancies between his or her self-concept as a teacher and what he or she actually sees on the tape (Perlberg 1983, p. 641; Tiberius 1995, p. 190). In teaching, as in much human behavior, many actions in routine situations become very spontaneous or automatic. "Deautomization involves redirecting one's attention onto those processes for which attention was no longer necessary once the behavior became 'automatized.' . . . Perhaps changes in entrenched spontaneous behaviors do not persist over time unless deautomatization takes place" (Fuller and Manning 1973, p. 483). Video self-confrontation has been found to be especially effective for improving instruction when it is used with a consultation. In reviewing a videotape, one of the consultant's primary tasks (in addition to creating a safe environment) is to focus the instructor's attention on specific teaching behaviors while viewing the tape (Perlberg 1983, p. 648).

The Role of the Department Chair
While helping faculty to develop has long been recognized as an important activity for the department chair, it has grown in importance over the past 10 to 15 years (Gmelch 1995; Gmelch and Miskin 1993; Lucas 1989, 1990, 1994; Seagren, Creswell, and Wheeler 1993; Tucker 1993; D. Wheeler 1992). The director of the Center for the Study of the Department Chair at Washington State University reports that "department chairs view their *faculty developer* role as their most important responsibility. . . . Ironically, chairs feel least trained and prepared in this area" (Gmelch 1995, p. 154).

Studies of the sources of stress and satisfaction for new and junior faculty highlight the importance of the chair as a faculty developer. Such studies have revealed that one of the primary sources of stress for new faculty is a lack of collegial support from senior faculty; however, one potential source of satisfaction is the crucial support that could be provided by the department chair (Boice 1992b; Sorcinelli 1988, 1992; Turner and Boice 1989; Whitt 1991). New faculty have identified department chairs as their advocates (Sorcinelli 1988) and their mentors (Turner and Boice 1989). Those department chairs "who were cited as particularly helpful seemed to take time to assign courses that fit [new faculty members'] interests and priorities" or worked "to negotiate minimal preps or a reduced load" for newer faculty (Sorcinelli 1994, p. 475). A relatively recent qualitative investigation of the experiences of new faculty and the role of the department chair was based on 21 interviews with six new faculty and on interviews with six department chairs and four administrators on the dean's staff at a large research university (Whitt 1991). Some new faculty praised their chairs for the concern and help they provided; others complained that their chairs were not as helpful as they should have been. Administrators described the role of the chair as "critical" to the support of new faculty, explaining that "the department chair's attitude is key—an attitude that it is part of the job of the chair to provide unusual support for the new faculty to make sure that they become good teachers, establish a meaningful program of research, and receive honest feedback and praise" (p. 186). Likewise, in an evaluation of the Lilly Teaching Fellows Program, interview data showed that an important source of support for participating faculty regarding their teaching came from the encouragement and recognition they received from their department chairs. Researchers concluded that without "the support of department chairs, many incentives to encourage good teaching may be fruitless" (Rice and Austin 1990, p. 39).

How important is the chair in instructional improvement?

In a relatively recent national survey of faculty developers, respondents were asked to indicate which activities for improving instruction were currently available on their campuses and which of them they themselves desired or planned to implement. The most "desirable" of all activities for improving instruction was training department chairs to be facilitators of such improvement. Researchers concluded that "the strongest indicator of interest in new collaborative efforts is the high proportion of respondents (60 percent) who report that they would like to work with chairs to facilitate teaching improvement, compared with the low percentage who currently do so (16 percent)" (Kurfiss and Boice 1990, p. 80). A recent international survey of 331 faculty developers asked respondents to rate 36 practices for improving teaching according to their potential to improve the quality of teaching (Wright and O'Neil 1995). Three of the practices ranked in the top 10 across the entire sample (including the United States, Canada, the United Kingdom, and Australasia) directly involved department chairs. "Teaching is fostered as an important aspect of academic responsibility by deans and department heads" was ranked second overall, and "Good teaching is praised and rewarded by deans and department heads" was ranked eighth overall and fifth in the U.S. sample. "Climate of trust created by deans and department heads [that] supports classroom observation" was ranked fourth overall. This finding indicates the very high confidence that faculty developers have in the positive impact on teaching of the collegial coaching and team teaching projects discussed earlier. While faculty developers perceive themselves "as the campus 'experts' on teaching," the results of this survey also indicate their "belief in the capacity of faculty members to provide one another with meaningful feedback and advice on teaching with minimal guidance from central agencies" (Wright and O'Neil 1995, p. 15). Finally, in support of the chair's importance in instructional improvement, a study of 300 faculty at 15 colleges and universities (as discussed earlier) reveals that the most important determinant of whether an academic department has a supportive teaching culture is the department chair's role "in creating an environment conducive to effective teaching" (Massy, Wilger, and Colbeck 1994, p. 17).

This finding indicates the very high confidence that faculty developers have in the positive impact on teaching of the collegial coaching and team teaching projects . . .

How do effective chairs promote improved instruction?

Based on research on the role of administrators in faculty development, department chairs are more likely than deans to become actively involved in assisting faculty in their development, and "their involvement usually focuses on teaching improvement" (Boice 1992b, p. 295). In the Department of Psychology at the University of Missouri–Columbia, the chair and associate chair define faculty development and instructional improvement as a departmental activity (DiLorenzo and Heppner 1994). They have developed a successful faculty peer consultation program for instructional improvement, which, framed as completely distinct from the evaluation of faculty, is an example of the type of departmental programs in which faculty developers expressed their confidence in the international survey described earlier (Wright and O'Neil 1995). The program is an application of collegial coaching that engages faculty pairs in observing each other's classes, interviewing each other's students, writing reports of information derived from both sources, and sharing feedback and ideas for improvement in consultative sessions (Heppner and Johnston 1994). These techniques are similar to those discussed under collegial coaching and consultation in this section and those discussed under "talking with students" in the previous one.

A department chair at Fairleigh Dickinson University recently described how she was able to introduce observations in the classroom by colleagues (for improvement) into a department when she joined the department both as a new faculty member and the new chair (Lucas 1994). Several senior faculty, who were excellent teachers, complained that they should do something to improve the "very poor" teaching of some untenured faculty. In the chair's previous department, peer observation had been the norm; therefore, it was her first recommendation. The senior faculty told her, "We don't do colleague observation in this department, but if Harry and I volunteer to have you visit our classes, then it won't seem as if you are just observing the worst people in the department" (p. 106). She observed these two senior and excellent teachers first, and it helped her to make classroom observation a new departmental norm.

As described earlier, a technique that more department chairs are beginning to use is one of a number of variations of the pedagogical colloquium. The alternative formats for the pedagogical colloquium (a course narrative or course argument approach, a colloquium centered on an essential idea or concept, or a dilemma-centered colloquium) provide efficient and effective means of embedding an assessment of teaching effectiveness into the process of hiring new faculty (Byrnes 1995; Shulman 1995).

When a University of Wisconsin professor became the chair of his department, he routinely received and reviewed the syllabi developed by all the faculty in the department. As he examined the other professors' syllabi, he began to rethink some of the teaching approaches he used in his own classes. It was such an eye-opening experience for him that he "gathered and distributed copies of everyone's course syllabi . . . [and] soon discovered that this sharing process encouraged everyone to be much more thoughtful about course planning and the preparation of teaching materials" (Trask 1989, p. 102).

In a study of 30 department chairs who were recommended for the study as a result of their effectiveness in faculty development, participants were asked to talk about what they had done to help faculty members develop (Wilhite 1990; Wilhite and Leininger 1988). A general pattern of effective practices used to help troubled faculty emerged from the interview data. Chairs tried to anticipate problems by interacting frequently with and monitoring the performance of their faculty. When specific problems were identified, the chair and instructor worked together to develop a strategy that capitalized on the strengths of the individual; the chair encouraged and supported the faculty members in their efforts to change.

Another, larger study was based on interviews with 200 department chairs at 75 institutions. The chairs were recommended by senior administrators or faculty development specialists on their campuses, based on their distinguished records of developmental work with their faculty (Creswell, Wheeler, Seagren, Egly, and Beyer 1990). The researchers asked chairs to describe what they did to improve the teaching performance of their faculty. They used the results of their interview data to suggest that "excellent" chairs follow a set of steps similar to a comprehensive process of instructional consultation (Bergquist and Phillips 1977; Povlacs 1988): gather background information; clarify the goals and objectives; observe the performance yourself; facilitate improvement and the practice of new skills; and monitor progress toward improvement and advocate for the individual (Creswell et al. 1990, pp. 61–67). A specific case, such as the following one, illustrates this process. In this case, the teacher was a new professor in an education department. She had excellent research skills but needed to work on her teaching.

1. *Gather background information.* During the first year, the chair "just spent time sitting in her office, talking to her, and not doing much." But the chair also visited with students about complaints and reviewed carefully the students' evaluations.
2. *Clarify the problem.* By the end of the second year, it was necessary to begin taking steps to improve the individual's teaching. The chair and the faculty member visited and began thinking about a faculty development plan and carried out several activities under the plan.
3. *Observe the performance yourself.* The chair videotaped the faculty member's teaching in a few classes and then reviewed with the individual the strengths and weaknesses of her teaching. Together, they isolated teaching behaviors that needed improvement. Then the chair sat in on a couple of her classes to observe her.
4. *Facilitate improvement and practice.* The chair and the faculty member team taught a course together that required that both of them attend every session. Finally, the dean provided a summer faculty development grant so that the chair and the faculty member could spend three weeks during the summer modifying one of her courses.
5. *Monitor progress.* Over a period of several years, the chair monitored students' evaluations. By the sixth year, teaching had improved: "She had gone from approximately a 1.5 on a five-point scale (five as a high point) to a 4.1 or 4.2 in the intervening years." At the end of her sixth year, she was given tenure (pp. 67–68).

Faculty developers at the University of Minnesota–Duluth describe a special training program that they use to prepare departmental faculty to comfortably and effectively observe each other's classes to improve instruction (Hilsen and Rutherford 1991). It is a comprehensive program in which the chair serves as facilitator, helping faculty to get an overview of the entire training process; discuss the difference between peer observation (for improvement only) and peer evaluation (for personnel decisions); discuss openly the anxieties of both tenured and untenured faculty working together to improve teaching; use video to see the difference between focused, descriptive observation and random, judgmental observation; discover the value systems underly-

*Evidence is increasing that new and junior faculty find
the initial years in academe to be a time of great stress
as well as satisfaction. On the one hand, new and
junior faculty enjoy flexibility in how they do their
work, opportunities to learn and grow, and pleasures
from interacting with students and engaging in their
scholarly work. On the other hand, they often are frus-
trated by insufficient time to fulfill all demands, difficulty in establishing supportive collegial relationships,
insufficient resources, fear of nonreappointment, and
struggles in balancing work and personal life. . . .
Research also suggests that new and junior faculty need
assistance on several fronts and that colleagues and
administrators need to better understand how junior
faculty develop careers and cope with career pressures.
In fact, the willingness of institutions to learn about
and provide support during the early years may be vital
to their ability to attract and retain potential faculty
members* (Sorcinelli and Austin 1992, p. 1).

Although supportive teaching cultures and effective informative feedback from a variety of sources are generally beneficial for the improvement of instruction, specific tailoring
may be needed for certain categories. One such group comprises new and junior faculty.

New and junior faculty refer to "nontenured, full-time
faculty below the rank of associate professor, including
some who are new to the profession, some who are new to
their current institution of employment, and some who are
in the midst of probationary appointments" (Finkelstein and
LaCelle-Peterson 1992, p. 8). Today's new faculty differ from
earlier generations in several ways: They have obtained
positions in a competitive academic marketplace, a larger
proportion are women, their average age is greater, a larger
proportion represent dual-career households, and a larger
proportion hold degrees from the more elite research institutions. By the end of this century, two factors are expected to
work in combination to generate a substantial increase in
demand for new and junior faculty—retirements of a large
number of faculty hired during the boom of the late 1960s
and early 1970s and increases in higher education enrollment (Finkelstein and LaCelle-Peterson 1992). The following
subsections examine the experiences of new and junior

faculty that characterize academic careers during the pre-tenure years, the socialization of new faculty, institutional programs for the orientation of new and junior faculty, and mentoring programs that facilitate collegial support for junior faculty through professional interactions with senior faculty. The latter two subsections emphasize their implications for instructional improvement.

Experiences of New and Junior Faculty

A number of scholars have employed adult development theories (see, e.g., Levinson 1986) to conceptualize and study faculty careers (Baldwin 1979, 1990; Baldwin and Blackburn 1981; Blackburn 1979, 1985; Braskamp, Fowler, and Ory 1984; Cytrynbaum, Lee, and Wadner 1982; Furniss 1981; Hodgkinson 1974; Mathis 1979; Menges 1985). Various sequences of developmental stages have been expressed in terms of a "generic view" of the academic career that includes four phases: novice professor, early academic career, midcareer, and late career (Baldwin 1990). The earli-est stage of a faculty member's career—the novice profes-sor—happens during the pretenure years and portrays the experiences, tasks, concerns, and developmental needs of new and junior faculty. A primary need of the novice profes-sor is to establish competence. A most pressing concern is the development of a repertoire of effective teaching skills. Among the tasks to be performed first are the design of a number of new courses, often in particular subjects that are not within the new professor's primary areas of expertise. It is often necessary for the new faculty member to carry out these demanding teaching tasks while establishing an appro-priate research agenda. Further, each of these professional demands must be met in the face of competing responsibili-ties in one's personal life. In all, then, this stage is a time of intense pressure and stress. During this time of transition into an academic career, the new faculty member might be assisted through institutional resources and support in the form of a campus teaching center, orientations, supportive department chairs, and mentoring (Baldwin 1990, pp. 31–33). A successful transition or socialization during this early phase is especially important for the faculty career; that is, "the problems and performance of novice faculty mem-bers influence their later occupational progress" (Baldwin 1979, p. 17).

Studies of new faculty careers have revealed a number of common themes that characterize the experiences of new and junior faculty during the pretenure years. Whether at liberal arts colleges or large research universities, new faculty are enthusiastic about their jobs (Baldwin and Blackburn 1981; Sorcinelli 1988), but they also agree that this early phase of their careers is a particularly stressful time of their lives (Baldwin and Blackburn 1981; Braskamp, Fowler, and Ory 1984; Menges 1994; see also Ratcliff and Associates 1995). One of the primary sources of stress is a perceived lack of sufficient time for their activities. Time constraints make it very difficult to balance the competing demands of teaching, research, and service, and limit opportunities to meet the responsibilities associated with personal, social, and family life (Sorcinelli 1988; Sorcinelli and Near 1989). New faculty often describe themselves as being "the busiest they've ever been in their lives" (Turner and Boice 1989, p. 53), and a typical strategy for coping is to "work harder, faster, and longer" (Sorcinelli 1988, p. 124). Moreover, longitudinal analysis indicates that the stress associated with these difficulties intensifies as the time for tenure review approaches (Olsen and Sorcinelli 1992).

Although new faculty are committed to teaching well, they are often inadequately prepared to teach effectively (Boice 1991b; Sorcinelli 1988), express concerns about how to teach better (Baldwin and Blackburn 1981; Stanley and Chism 1991; Turner and Boice 1987), and often receive unsatisfactory ratings of their teaching (Fink 1984; Turner and Boice 1987). The lion's share of new faculty's work time is spent on preparation for teaching (Boice 1991b), and they spend significantly more time on teaching than their senior colleagues (Fairweather and Rhoads 1995; Olsen, Maple, and Stage 1995). The primary reason new faculty spend so much time on teaching is that they persistently overprepare. "New faculty in their first three years at large campuses expended surprising amounts of time in lecture preparation: Norms for new faculty with two-course-per-semester assignments were 13 to 22 hours per week; with three-course loads, 18 to 27 hours" (Boice 1991c, p. 112). Other reasons new faculty spend particularly large amounts of time on their teaching include the need to develop new courses, a high number of separate preparations, and large classes (Boice 1991b; Fink 1984; Sorcinelli 1988; Turner and Boice 1989).

The most common approach to teaching among new faculty is dominated by the lecture or "knowledge-oriented principles-and-facts prototype," a style modeled after their own professors (Fink 1984, p. 101). They commonly consider good teaching to mean "clear, knowledgeable, and, possibly, inspiring lectures" (Boice 1991b, p. 157), and they rarely have plans to improve their teaching, other than preparing better lectures and reducing standards of difficulty. In a study of 66 new faculty during their first year at a large state university, the most common approach to teaching often resulted "in a syndrome [that] might be termed 'assistant professoritis'—i.e., new faculty overprepare, feel compelled to teach everything they know, provide little time or incentive for student participation, impress students as aloof and unapproachable, receive poor student evaluations, and blame this outcome on the poor quality of students in their classes" (Turner and Boice 1987, p. 44).

A recent qualitative investigation of the experiences of 45 new faculty during their first five years at a large research university, however, revealed that by their fifth year, new faculty experience a significant improvement in the efficiency of their preparation for lectures, receive higher evaluations from students, become more introspective about aspects of their teaching, express greater confidence in their teaching abilities, and become more satisfied with their teaching experiences (Olsen and Sorcinelli 1992). Additionally, a study of 106 faculty at 12 liberal arts colleges found a substantial improvement in the "rating of comfortableness with teaching" between new faculty in their first three years and those in their second three years as an assistant professor (Baldwin and Blackburn 1981, p. 605).

In a relatively recent longitudinal study, four cohorts of new faculty—two cohorts from a teaching-oriented university and two cohorts from a research-oriented university—were interviewed in successive semesters about their teaching and related work experiences (Boice 1991b, 1991c, 1992b). A set of common characteristics of the teaching approaches of new faculty members emerged from the interview data:

1. They rely primarily on a facts-and-principles type of lecturing and conceive of good teaching as meaning good content;

2. They think of their facts-and-principles style of lecturing as a means of defense against complaints from students that might give senior colleagues the impression that they do not know their material;
3. They attribute their unsatisfactory student ratings to external factors, such as the poor quality of students, heavy teaching loads, or invalid student rating systems;
4. They are usually inactive regarding instructional change or improvement, are reluctant to seek assistance from campus teaching centers, and limit plans for improvement to preparing better lecture content and making assignments easier;
5. They do not even expect to really enjoy teaching or move beyond their facts-and-principles approach to teaching (for example, toward teaching critical thinking) until they find that they no longer need to spend so much time in preparation or to worry about criticisms;
6. Even those with prior teaching experience at other campuses use a facts-and-principles style of lecturing as a defense against students' criticism, describing the practice as a temporary regression from how they had recently taught at other campuses; and
7. They reach the point of being comfortable and efficient in their teaching or achieve acceptance from students either very slowly or not at all, although they become somewhat more efficient in preparing lectures by the fourth year and those few who persist as participants in programs sponsored by the campus teaching center progress in more aspects of their teaching (Boice 1991b, pp. 170–71).

As this profile indicates, "many of the initial habits of new faculty seem less than ideal . . . [, and] this . . . disheartening pattern . . . probably holds true on a variety of campuses" (Boice 1991c, pp. 111–12). Based on superior ratings from students, observers' ratings of performance in the classroom, and faculty self-ratings, however, several new faculty from each cohort were identified as exemplary teachers or "quick starters" on their respective campuses. The following characteristics distinguish them from their new peers and suggest ways in which other new faculty can be helped to become better teachers.

1. They have positive attitudes about their students;

2. They lecture in a relaxed style and provide opportunities for students to comprehend the material and become involved in the class;
3. They exhibit low levels of complaining about lack of collegial support;
4. They actively seek advice about their teaching from senior colleagues in the role of a mentor;
5. They quickly need only moderate levels of time to prepare lectures;
6. They spend a substantial amount of time on scholarly and grant writing; and
7. They are readier to become involved in campus faculty development programs (Boice 1991b, p. 169).

One of the most persistent and prevalent sources of stress for new faculty is their concern over the lack of collegiality—primarily, the inadequacy of encouragement and assistance from senior colleagues—that they experience compared to what they need and expected during their pretenure years (Boice 1991b; Fink 1984; Sorcinelli 1988; Whitt 1991). In a study of 66 new faculty in their first year at a large state university, new faculty "anticipated an intellectually stimulating and supportive environment with frequent informal interactions about scholarly issues, teaching, and other professional matters. They expected their senior colleagues to be active mentors who would serve as good role models and as a source of constructive advice and encouragement" (Turner and Boice 1987, p. 43). And in another study of 54 faculty in their first year at a large research university, this lack of assistance and support from senior colleagues was "the most surprising and disappointing aspect of their first year" (Sorcinelli 1988, p. 126).

In a two-year study of four cohorts of new teachers, the advice offered by senior colleagues to new faculty was found to be primarily based on "gossip and politics," with only 3 to 6 percent of successive new faculty cohorts reporting any advice related to teaching (Boice 1991b, p. 154). New faculty reported some increase in the quantity of collegial interactions during their second year, but those "inexperienced newcomers who found collegial support for teaching got it from other new faculty. . . . 'It's like the blind leading the blind'" (Boice 1992b, p. 67). When new faculty members' experiences with collegial support were studied over four years, faculty reported both higher levels of support and less need for such support over the four years, but the "quality of collegial advice" did not improve over the four years and still primarily consisted of "the gossip/politics-laden information" that characterized such interactions during their first year (Boice 1991a, p. 40). One study found that new faculty members' satisfaction with collegial support decreases as they approach the time for tenure, and they tend to rate "colleagues outside their departments as most helpful or supportive of their careers, with untenured faculty and chairpersons as next most supportive, respectively" (Olsen and Sorcinelli 1992, p. 21).

Unfortunately, in the face of a lack of initiative from senior faculty and in spite of their desire for interaction with senior colleagues, most new faculty are reluctant to seek advice about their teaching and other professional matters (Boice 1991b; Turner and Boice 1987; Whitt 1991). "Some expressed concerns about sounding naive, unprofessional, or disorganized by asking for help from senior faculty: 'If I say anything, they might wonder if I'm really doing my job,' a big risk to take with those who make decisions about tenure" (Whitt 1991, p. 183). As noted earlier, however, new faculty identified as excellent teachers and quick starters have been found to approach a lack of collegial support without complaint; instead, they actively seek counsel about their teaching from senior colleagues in the role of mentor (Boice 1991b, 1991c, 1992b).

At some colleges, it could be more than just the quick starters who actively seek help from senior colleagues. Interview data from a recent two-year study of 31 new faculty at a comprehensive university (Branch 1995) reveal an interesting pattern of collegiality between junior and senior faculty that helps focus attention on the importance of this collegiality. New faculty were highly proactive in seeking advice from senior faculty about their teaching. Over 80 percent of the new faculty in the study reported seeking advice about teaching from their senior colleagues. Seventy-five percent of the new faculty spoke at length about their plans for instructional improvement, and when they discussed those plans, they frequently referred to the consultative sessions they had experienced with senior colleagues. The results of the study indicate that "the emphasis placed on teaching . . . combined with the relatively high levels of

. . . in the face of a lack of initiative from senior faculty and in spite of their desire for interaction with senior colleagues, most new faculty are reluctant to seek advice about their teaching and other professional matters.

collegial support on campus, did appear to be influencing the new faculty's attitudes toward their teaching" (p. 216). In combination, these findings (Boice 1991b; Branch 1995) appear to suggest that the socialization of new faculty and ultimately the quality of their teaching could both be related to the level of interaction about teaching between junior and senior faculty.

The Socialization of New Faculty

Socialization can be defined as "the process by which individuals acquire the attitudes, beliefs, values, and skills needed to participate effectively in organized social life" (Dunn, Rouse, and Seff 1994, p. 375). More specifically, organizational socialization "refers to the manner in which the experiences of people learning the ropes of a new organizational position, status, or role are structured for them by others within the organization" (Van Maanen 1978, p. 19). Interviews with department chairs and dean's staff administrators at a major research university reveal that "they expected new faculty to already know a great deal about being a faculty member, to be experienced researchers and teachers, to have values and goals consistent with their new institution, and to . . . 'hit the ground running'" (Whitt 1991, p. 185). Yet when new faculty were asked "What is it like to be a new faculty member?" they responded with statements like "I have no idea what's going on," "I get no messages from this place," and "I feel I've been thrown into a big pool without knowing how to swim" (p. 189). The "experiences of this particular group of new faculty would lead [one] to speculate that having to be responsible for their own socialization may have added to the already heavy workload of new faculty" (p. 193).

Some research suggests that the socialization of new faculty "operates on social Darwinistic principles; as one inexperienced new assistant professor commented, 'Just as graduate schools let many students sink or swim in the dissertation stage, we also seem to willingly let people, even good people, fail . . . if they don't figure things out on their own'" (Boice 1992b, p. 44). The lack of institutional help in the form of structured opportunities for organizational socialization of new faculty could help explain why new faculty experience high levels of stress during their pretenure years (Dunn, Rouse, and Seff 1994). A recent review of the literature recommends a number of strategies or structures to promote the organizational socialization of new faculty; prominent among them are orientation and mentoring programs for new faculty (Austin and Sorcinelli 1992).

Orientation and mentoring programs—whose description and analysis take up the rest of this section—can be conceived of as two types of structures for organizational socialization of new faculty. They can be characterized and their benefits better understood in terms of several tactical dimensions of organizational socialization (Van Maanen and Schein 1979): collective versus individual structures; formal versus informal structures; and serial versus disjunctive structures (p. 232; see also S. Wheeler 1966).

Collective approaches to socialization place newcomers in a group and provide them with a common set of experiences. In contrast, *individual* approaches socialize newcomers by isolating them from one another, resulting in a relatively distinct set of experiences for each person. The individual approach typically dominates the socialization of new faculty in the great majority of colleges and universities (Dunn, Rouse, and Seff 1994, pp. 393–94; Tierney and Rhoads 1993, p. 27). Research on the experiences of new faculty clearly shows, however, that they share a common set of concerns, especially during their first one or two years. During a collective socialization experience, "the thoughts, feelings, and actions of those in the recruit group almost always reflect an 'in the same boat' consciousness. Individual changes in perspective are therefore built upon an understanding of the problems faced by all group members" (Van Maanen and Schein 1979, p. 233). Because new faculty do share common concerns about such things as workload and stress from multiple demands, uncertainty about what is expected of them, a desire for collegial support, and a need to develop teaching skills (Austin and Sorcinelli 1992), a strong argument can be made for supplementing the traditional, individual approaches to socialization with a collective approach that addresses these common concerns. Orientations (workshops) for new faculty that offer concrete assistance with the development of teaching skills and address other common concerns of new faculty are being used successfully in a variety of college and university settings (Fink 1992).

During *formal* approaches to socialization, newcomers are separated from the regular work setting and put through a tailored set of learning experiences. The formal socialization of new faculty is represented primarily by extensive graduate school training and teaching assistantships (Dunn, Rouse, and Seff 1994, p. 392) that constitute the bulk of "anticipatory socialization" preceding organizational socialization for new faculty (Tierney and Rhoads 1993, p. 23). *Informal* socialization is based on a laissez-faire approach that requires newcomers to learn from experience—trial and error—in the regular work setting, "where they must select their own socialization agents . . . [and] must force others in the setting to teach them" (Van Maanen and Schein 1979, p. 238).

The organizational socialization of new faculty relies primarily on informal approaches, and "at a minimum, new faculty need experienced and caring mentors" (Tierney and Rhoads 1993, p. 28). A recent study of the experiences of four cohorts of new faculty—two from a comprehensive university and two from a research university—reveals that women and minority faculty reported significantly fewer instances of "substantial mentoring" than their white male peers, even though "there were no fewer offers of mentoring for nontraditional newcomers than for men" (Boice 1993, p. 306). This lack of mentoring for women and minority faculty could be because they are underrepresented in the professoriat and because, while "majority-group senior faculty can mentor women and minorities, it is more difficult for these mentors to be role models. . . . Furthermore, mentors who have navigated nontraditional paths can provide specific information on how they overcame the obstacles associated with token status" (Dunn, Rouse, and Seff 1994, pp. 401–2).

In *serial* socialization, a senior member of the organization serves as a role model or mentor for a newcomer to assist him or her in successfully assuming a similar organizational position. But "when no role models are available to recruits to inform them as to how they are to proceed in the new role, the socialization process is a *disjunctive* one . . . [and] such situations make things extremely difficult and anxiety-provoking for the newcomer" (Van Maanen and Schein 1979, pp. 247–48). Mentoring programs for new faculty can offer concrete assistance with the development of teaching skills and address other of their professional and personal concerns (Sorcinelli 1995).

Orientation of New Faculty

Eighty-nine percent of the respondents in a relatively recent survey of 155 faculty development professionals indicated that they either currently use or plan to use "orientations on teaching skills for new faculty" as a strategy for instructional improvement on their campuses (Kurfiss and Boice 1990, p. 77). In an international survey of 331 faculty developers in the United States (N = 165), Canada (N = 51), the United Kingdom (N = 82), and Australasia (N = 33), "workshops on teaching methods for targeted groups, such as new faculty and teaching assistants," were ranked seventh out of 36 strategies for instructional improvement in terms of their potential to improve the quality of teaching (Wright and O'Neil 1995, p. 33).

Several possible reasons exist for the perceived value of orientation and mentoring in instructional improvement of new faculty. First, for the most part, graduate schools still do not assume the responsibility for effectively preparing future faculty in terms of pedagogical skills. Second, institutions assume that new faculty can indeed be motivated to improve their teaching during the pretenure years as part of their preparation for the tenure decision. Third, much like teaching assistants, most new faculty members encounter a common set of challenges regarding the improvement of their effectiveness in teaching (Weimer and Lenze 1991, pp. 319–20). Finally, research shows that at least four persistent needs of new faculty can be addressed by such programs— the need to develop teaching skills, the need for collegiality, the need for information about institutional expectations and resources, and the need to reduce stress from the multiple demands of teaching, research, and service (Austin and Sorcinelli 1992, pp. 97–98).

A study of 100 new faculty during their first year of teaching reveals that these first-year teachers struggled with having a limited range of teaching skills, experienced limited interaction with their colleagues, and complained of a frustrating and stressful workload. When asked what institutions could do to help new faculty, however, they responded most frequently that institutions should provide "better information at the start of the year" (Fink 1984, p. 107). Orientation as discussed here refers to something other than common and brief welcome-to-campus sessions offering information on fringe benefits, parking stickers, campus facilities, institutional policies, and the like. It refers to "substantial orientation programs" (Fink 1992, p. 41) or "teaching effectiveness workshops" (Eison and Hill 1990, p. 225) for new faculty, which include essential campus and institutional information but also give significant attention to the development of classroom teaching skills and other professional responsibilities of new faculty (research and grant writing, for example). Among the "lessons learned the hard way" by faculty developers at Southeast Missouri State University was that new faculty need to receive fundamental campus and institutional information as an important part of an orientation "before [they] become willing to think about [effective teaching]" (Renegar, Summary, Bonwell, and Eison 1987, p. 117). Although meeting these immediate needs of new faculty is necessary, however, it "does little to close the gap between subject matter expertise and teaching effectiveness" (Eison and Hill 1990, p. 225). In the early 1980s, faculty developers at the University of Texas, because of their concern about filling this gap, prepared a weeklong orientation that focused more on basic teaching skills for new faculty:

> *It always has seemed peculiar, and a little backward, that elementary and secondary teachers are provided with training in teaching skills as well as content matter while college instructors are very seldom, if ever, exposed to methods [that] will assist them in guiding the learning of their students. This lack of specific training in teaching techniques can be extremely stressful for a new faculty member as well as inefficient as they try to learn "on the job"* (Lewis, Svinicki, and Stice 1985, p. 16).

This situation raises an important challenge for higher education—one that substantial orientations for new faculty can effectively address. Such orientations can be described along several dimensions: (1) *timing*—is it offered before the fall semester or periodically over the course of the first semester or year? (2) *content*—what is the relative emphasis of the orientation on teaching, research, and institutional information? (3) *attendance*—is it mandatory or voluntary? (4) *audience*—does it include only full-time faculty or part-time faculty as well? (5) *organization*—does the university hold one common or centralized orientation for all new faculty or are there decentralized programs for new faculty in different colleges or departments? (Fink 1992, p. 41).

One of the earliest large-scale programs for orienting new faculty was undertaken at the University of Texas at Austin, beginning in 1980 (Lewis, Svinicki, and Stice 1985). The program was initially offered during the full week just before fall registration but has since been shortened to three days (Erickson 1992); its content is primarily related to teaching but also includes information about the campus and the community (Erickson 1992; Fink 1992). Attendance is voluntary, all new faculty are invited, the program is centralized, and it is designed and facilitated primarily by the campus teaching center. An extensive packet of written materials (250 pages) supplements the program, and many experienced faculty are involved as presenters at various sessions. Participants have many opportunities to interact with each other. Early in the orientation, institutional rules and regulations are explained, and participants complete all formal personnel forms together. The first aspects of teaching to be addressed are designing courses and syllabi and becoming acquainted with the university's students. During the middle part of the program, new faculty choose from a variety of sessions on teaching methods presented by experienced faculty who actually use these methods in their teaching. The latter part of the program covers evaluation of teaching, instructional improvement, and the campus teaching center's activities; it also includes presentations on communication and learning theories underlying the teaching methods covered in previous sessions. According to participants, the two strongest points of the orientation are the "chance to meet and interact with various faculty members from other disciplines" and the emphasis of the program "on teaching[, which] helps them prepare themselves and their materials for a more productive beginning in their new positions" (Lewis, Svinicki, and Stice 1985, p. 20).

The campus teaching center at Southeast Missouri State University offers a centralized, weeklong program modeled after the orientation program at Texas for new faculty during the week before the fall semester. Unlike the program at Texas, however, this program is for full-time faculty only, and attendance is mandatory (Renegar et al. 1987). The major topics covered in the sessions (as well as in a supplementary reference book) include designing courses, teaching critical thinking, leading discussions, lecturing effectively, and constructing tests. In response to feedback from participants, a number of noteworthy improvements have been made over the years (Eison 1989). Department chairs are asked to distribute letters to all job applicants indicating that participation in the orientation for new faculty is expected if they accept the position. Additionally, a short statement has been added to contracts for new faculty that addresses the requirement of attendance. After the contract is signed, new faculty receive letters from the provost and the director of the campus teaching center that describe the program. New faculty are also surveyed regarding their interests in various instructional topics. Extensive information about the campus (tours of the campus and library are also offered) and the community is now provided on the first day of the orientation, and two-hour lunch periods and all of Wednesday are now set aside for participants to attend to other responsibilities during the week before classes begin. Participants now choose among alternative sessions, small-group sessions now permit more interaction among participants, active learning techniques are used more extensively, and participants evaluate each session separately.

Other successful orientation programs include aspects similar to these two models, but each has one or more features that make it distinctive. The orientation program for new faculty at the State University of New York at Buffalo, for example, is a centralized four-day program offered two weeks before fall classes begin; attendance is voluntary and limited to full-time faculty (Welch, Solkoff, Schimpfhauser, and Henderson 1988). A special feature of the program is that about one-third of the total time is devoted to micro-teaching in small groups; this experience gives "participants an opportunity to receive *immediate* corrective feedback from peers of videotaped, eight- to 10-minute lecture segments" (p. 110). Orientation at the University of Oklahoma is a centralized program for all new faculty members (attendance is voluntary) that consists of a semester-long set of weekly 75-minute luncheon seminars. The content focuses on professional development (rather than just instructional development) and covers issues related to research, teaching, and university resources (Fink 1992). At Luther College in Iowa, orientation consists of "advance readings, a one-day general orientation, and a program of weekly discussions with follow-up newsletters through the fall semester" (Jakoubek 1994, p. 226). Topics for the weekly discussions are chosen by the new faculty, a senior faculty member is asked to be a resource person on each week's topic, and a one-page newsletter summarizes the key points and practical suggestions that emerge from each week's discussion. The components of these successful orientations are consistent with a set of suggested program goals based on a national survey of 69 faculty developers with experience in designing and conducting orientations and workshops for new faculty (Eison and Hill 1990). One additional program goal identified in the survey is noteworthy: "development of a mentoring program for new faculty" (p. 227).

Mentoring Programs

A number of scholars have responded to the needs of new faculty to develop their teaching abilities and increase their interaction with senior colleagues by recommending mentoring programs that would develop teaching and other professional knowledge and skills (Austin and Sorcinelli 1992; Cox 1995; Jarvis 1991; Sorcinelli 1994, 1995; Turner and Boice 1987, 1989). Among desired or planned strategies for improving instruction, a larger percentage of 155 faculty developers in one survey recommended "recruiting senior faculty as mentors of teaching for new faculty" than any other strategy except "training department chairs to facilitate teaching" (Kurfiss and Boice 1990, pp. 76–77). A recent international survey of 331 faculty developers reveals that "mentoring programs [that] include such activities as peer consultation and faculty support systems for new professors" was rated fifth out of 36 strategies in potential to improve the quality of teaching (Wright and O'Neil 1995, pp. 35–36). Mentoring programs discussed in this subsection emphasize the improvement of teaching.

The Lilly Endowment Teaching Fellows Program is arguably the most well known and one of the most effective overall programs for assisting new faculty in improving their teaching (Austin 1990b, 1992). A significant number of these programs have contained an embedded, formal mentoring program—some 12 of the 16 that reported the components of their programs (Austin 1990b). The pattern of senior-junior faculty mentoring varies across programs. Generally, senior faculty mentors are those who have an established campus reputation as excellent teachers and scholars. In some programs, new faculty are encouraged to select a mentor from a department other than their own to protect them from any experiences or issues that might prejudice decisions about tenure. In other programs, new faculty are encouraged to select a mentor who is from the same department so that they share the perspective of their discipline, meetings can be easily arranged, and the mentor can be on hand to protect the mentee from excessive departmental workloads while they are working together. Another common pattern is to allow new faculty to select their mentors either from their own department or from a different department.

The mentor's role also varies across programs. "Some pairs arrange regular meetings to discuss teaching-related issues and to visit each other's classes. There are some instances where a mentor and fellow have engaged in joint research projects. . . . In some programs, mentors also meet separately with the program directors for orientation to their roles and responsibilities" (Austin 1992, p. 77). When it comes to arrangements for mentoring in the Teaching Fellows Program, "one factor associated with success is . . . flexibility in approach" (p. 78).

A number of published reports of successful mentoring programs (that emphasize the improvement of teaching) are available in the literature. A Lilly Teaching Fellows Program with a successful mentoring component was held at the University of Florida (Austin 1990b). The teaching fellows were paired with mentors from their home departments and worked in an "apprenticeship relationship" to improve teaching. The pairs became "participant observers in each other's classes and talked frankly about successes and problems in their teaching" (p. 180).

The Teaching Improvement Program (TIPs) at the University of Georgia was developed largely in response to the ongoing success of its Lilly Teaching Fellows Program. TIPs "was conceived as a way of helping junior faculty by providing them with a senior faculty mentor" (Diehl and Simpson 1989, p. 149). Mentors are senior faculty members who are widely known to be outstanding teachers. Most mentors are winners of university teaching awards, members of the University Instructional Advisory Committee, or former mentors for Lilly Fellows. Initially, mentees included both faculty who were new to the university and had little teaching experience, and faculty who had previous teaching experience but were new to that university or were in their second year of teaching. Later, only new faculty without prior teaching experience were eligible to be mentees. Mentees are paired with mentors from a department other than their own to separate mentoring from decisions about tenure.

This program at the University of Georgia is administered by the campus teaching center (Office of Instructional Development). The associate director and director of the office describe the interactions between mentors and mentees as follows:

> *TIPs is designed for the mentor and mentee to meet two or three times over the course of a quarter. The first meeting, arranged by the TIPs staff, is a session to introduce the mentor and mentee. The next key meeting occurs when the mentor visits a class taught by the mentee. The mentor is instructed to observe the teaching performance and to be prepared to share observations with the mentee. The mentee is then invited to observe the teaching techniques of the mentor. The process is completed at a final meeting in which the mentor points out the strengths of the mentee's teaching and offers some suggestions on how classroom performance might be improved* (Jackson and Simpson 1994, p. 69).

This process of collegial coaching that constitutes the primary activity of TIPs has proven to be very effective. Even though some of the mentors have expressed concern that their suggestions for improvement—promoting discussion in class, setting expectations for the class, and trying new teaching methods—might not have been helpful, "the mentees reported those same suggestions to be very valuable" (Diehl and Simpson 1989, p. 154).

Mentoring has been an important component of Miami University's Teaching Scholars Program since 1978 (Cox 1995). Over the years, more than 125 senior faculty have offered to be mentors, each identifying specific areas of expertise in teaching. New faculty consult with their department chair and the program director to assist them in selecting an appropriate mentor from this list of volunteers, from an extended group that includes former teaching scholars and mentors, or from other colleagues with whom they would like to work. "The structure of their interaction is flexible: For example, the mentors and proteges may attend one another's classes, discuss teaching philosophies, or explore university issues together" (Cox 1994, pp. 81–82). Mentoring has also been a successful component of the Teaching Fellows Program (sponsored by the campus teaching center) at the University of Massachusetts at Amherst (Sorcinelli 1995). Much like Miami's program, interactions between mentors and mentees are varied. They might consist of mutual classroom observations, obtaining and discussing student feedback from each other's classes, and regular meetings to discuss teaching and other professional concerns. At Cardinal Stritch College in Milwaukee, each new faculty member is paired with a senior colleague, who serves as a mentor. In the first phase, they discuss teaching goals and methods and observe each other teach, while the department chair also observes the new faculty member's teaching. During the second phase, the mentor provides more services of a collegial coach. "The mentor and mentee review the chair's assessment of teaching, the students' rating, and their own evaluation of instruction. Their goal is to synthesize the diverse sources of feedback and to develop specific strategies for improvement and innovation" (Sorcinelli 1995, p. 130).

Some interesting variations on this common pattern reportedly have been effective. For example, the Senior Mentoring Service initiated at Temple University in 1990 offers each new full-time faculty member in the College of Arts and Sciences a mentor from a pool of recently retired faculty known for their excellence as teachers (Sorcinelli 1995). In addition to reviewing course materials with the mentee, the mentors "often visit proteges' classes or review a videotape of those classes" to facilitate their private discussions of teaching issues (p. 130). The University of Maryland University College administers a comprehensive faculty development program for its large cadre of part-time or adjunct instructors (about 60 each semester) (Millis 1994). Each new adjunct instructor is offered a teaching mentor, selected from a list of nominees for a university teaching award and current adjunct instructors with exceptionally high student ratings. These adjunct instructors "care about teaching, an avocation for them, and they welcome support" (p. 74).

A detailed and comprehensive two-year study of the nature and effectiveness of a systematic mentoring program involving 25 mentoring pairs at a large comprehensive university compared the activities and performance of new faculty who were participants in the formal mentoring program with new faculty who did not participate (had no mentors) and with a group of new faculty who did not participate in the program but were involved in spontaneous mentoring relationships unrelated to the formal program (Boice 1990). The structure of the formal mentoring program consisted of weekly meetings of each pair, monthly meetings of all pairs together, and biweekly meetings of pairs with the project director. Evaluation of the program included checklists completed by the pairs, describing topics and actions in each weekly meeting; ratings of the nature and effectiveness of each pair's interactions made by the director during biweekly meetings; interviews with participants at the beginning and end of the program; records of the conversation at monthly meetings of all pairs; overall scores of the effectiveness of mentoring on a mentoring index; personality assessments using the Myers-Briggs Type Indicator; and pairs' ongoing and end-of-year self-ratings of aspects of their experience (Boice 1990).

An overall finding of this study is that "all but a few of these pairs were highly successful. As a rule, mentoring was associated with more rapid socialization to campus and with improved student ratings of teaching compared to nonmentored peers" (Boice 1992a). The study has some other important findings:

1. Most of the mentoring pairs would not have persisted were it not for the "structure and prodding" provided in the formal project. "Every pair in the project volunteered this opinion at the end of a year, amid recollections of having initially disliked the recurring prods (via visits from the project director and via reports of activities and successes from other pairs in monthly group meetings) and structure (via data sheets and questionnaires)" (Boice 1990, p. 154);

". . . As a rule, mentoring was associated with more rapid socialization to campus and with improved student ratings of teaching compared to nonmentored peers."

2. Most of the content of interactions between mentoring pairs focused on two topics—teaching and scholarly productivity;
3. Getting mentors to become less passive and to assume an interventionist role (to supplement their roles as listener and supporter) in promoting instructional improvement required a tailored request from the project director: "Only when I structured the task of coaching mentees at teaching did mentors get more involved. They agreed, once involved, that brief visits to mentees' classes and subsequent feedback on a brief checklist could be managed in a constructive fashion. And they found that the practice of bringing their mentees to their own classes . . . was both helpful and reasonable" (Boice 1992a, p. 55);
4. Mentors who were arbitrarily paired were just as effective as those paired by department, gender, or ethnicity; and
5. Mentoring pairs shared a common conception and understanding of mentoring as "support and guidance in socializing new faculty" (Boice 1990, p. 150).

This research suggests that "a general principle for maximizing the usefulness of mentoring programs [is that] mentoring pairs may need considerable mentoring, including prods, directives, and chances to show off successes" (Boice 1992a, p. 55).

SUMMARY AND CONCLUSIONS

It is far from paradoxical to say that to understand how the teaching of *individual* faculty members can be improved, a good place to start is an examination of *organizational* forces within the university. The existing cultures, subcultures, and structural resources at universities in part condition the quality of instruction in classrooms and the ease or difficulty with which this quality can be changed. This report emphasizes not only the importance of increasing the quality of college teaching but also the great need for teaching cultures that encourage such efforts; in turn, the implementation of strategies to improve instruction helps create more supportive teaching cultures on college and university campuses.

Overview

Regardless of whether the teaching culture is the dominant culture or "merely" a subordinate subculture at a particular college or university, the characteristics of a culture that supports teaching are of great importance. The effectiveness of all strategies for improving instruction is clearly enhanced by the presence of a culture that is supportive of teaching. The relevant research literature, primarily qualitative studies, case studies, and surveys, has rather consistently identified the following characteristics of cultures that support teaching and its improvement:

- Unambiguous commitment and support by senior administrators to teaching and its improvement;
- Shared values about the importance of teaching between administrators and faculty, with the widespread involvement of faculty in planning and implementing activities and programs to improve teaching, thus creating a sense of the faculty's "ownership" of these activities and programs;
- A broad, expanded view of scholarship and scholarly activities;
- A requirement that some demonstration of effective teaching be part of interviewing and hiring new faculty;
- Frequent interaction and collaboration among faculty and a sense of community among faculty regarding teaching-related issues;
- A faculty development program or campus teaching center;

- Presence of effective department chairs who are supportive of teaching and its improvement;
- Decisions about tenure and promotion connected to rigorous evaluations of teaching.

This report has been particularly interested in the varieties of informative feedback—themselves facilitated by a supportive teaching culture—that drive the process of instructional improvement. Most strategies for improving instruction can be meaningfully arranged into categories according to the primary source of informative feedback that serves to initiate, direct, or sustain improvement in teaching. Prominent sources of such feedback are colleagues and consultants, chairs, students, and the teacher himself or herself.

With regard to, first, faculty colleagues as sources of informative feedback, faculty seminars, workshops, and colloquia are traditional (but still effective) practices for encouraging interaction and collaboration among faculty regarding teaching issues. Recent developments in a variety of areas—action science, reflective practice, adult learning theory, and the like—have encouraged an expanded range of strategies for improving instruction. One important set of activities, programs, and projects in this expansion is the renewed use of team teaching. Faculty collaboration through team teaching benefits professors by developing their teaching abilities, intellectually stimulating them, engaging them as self-directed learners, and more closely connecting them to the university or college as a community. The capacity of team teaching to improve instruction appears to derive from the opportunities for interaction provided by collaboration in teaching, through which colleagues come to trust one another, observe each other teach, and discuss their ideas and concerns about teaching. The various models of team teaching form a continuum from the least collaborative to the most collaborative. As far as can be told at this point, the most collaborative models seem to have the greatest success in improving teaching.

A second set of activities, programs, and projects that can be included in the expanded range of the use of faculty colleagues in improving instruction is collegial coaching. Two primary activities involved in collegial coaching are observation of classroom teaching and instructional consultation, including a review of course materials and discussions about classroom practices. Teachers who interact with their colleagues as coaches are using strategies for instructional improvement that engage them as self-directed learners. From the descriptions and analyses of coaching projects undertaken at a variety of colleges and universities, effective programs have all or most of the following attributes: (1) an underlying philosophy; (2) a procedure for selecting participants; (3) a training program for collegial coaches (observers/consultants); (4) a preobservation conference; (5) one or more classroom visits and observations; (6) a postobservation conference; and (7) participants' evaluations of their effectiveness.

Many of the informal processes of consultation carried out in collegial coaching projects have been formalized in a comprehensive set of more routine services provided by the trained consultants who constitute the staff of campus teaching centers. Instructional consultation is usually based on a comprehensive model that includes data collection and analysis by the consultant, strategies for improvement that are worked out between the consultant and the teacher, and evaluation. Consultation improves teaching primarily through the use of effective practices in giving feedback (often associated with student ratings and direct observation or videotapes of classroom teaching) and through the various interpersonal roles assumed by consultants (data collector, data manager, facilitator for instructional change, source of support to help analyze and interpret the results of trying new teaching behaviors, and information source about teaching and its improvement).

Chairs of departments, too, are important to the improvement of teaching. One way they help is by providing support—financial and otherwise—to ongoing formal and informal attempts to improve teaching. They can define faculty development and instructional improvement (as distinct from faculty evaluation) as important departmental activities. They can plan programs for the department, such as pedagogical colloquia, that help improve teaching. They can even intervene more directly by following a set of steps similar to those used in instructional consultation: gathering background information about the teaching of a member of the department; clarifying the teacher's goals and objectives; observing the teacher in the classroom; facilitating improvement and the practice of new skills; and monitoring progress toward improvement and advocating for the teacher.

Although it is sometimes forgotten, students are not "silent partners" in the enterprise of improving teaching. One way their voices can be heard is through filling out teacher and course evaluations. Research has shown persistently that feedback from students' ratings is of value in improving teaching, particularly if this feedback is accompanied by consultation with the teacher. Good evidence shows the utility of the teacher's sitting down with a colleague or teaching consultant to jointly interpret the feedback from students, select targets for improvement, and develop strategies for instructional change. And the more diagnostic the rating form used by students—for example, forms with items asking about specific or low-inference behaviors of teachers as contrasted with items about global or high-inference behaviors—the more help they are likely to be.

The voice of students can be heard even more directly by talking with them. Student interviews can be successfully used in several different ways to give feedback to teachers: group discussions; small-group instructional diagnosis; the class interview; and quality-control circles. A particularly distinctive way of receiving feedback from students is for a professor to invite students into his or her classroom who are not "official" members of the class but who are trained in classroom observation. The primary purpose of this approach is to provide confidential observations to increase the instructor's effectiveness in helping students learn. Another strategy for "listening" to students, "classroom assessment," comprises a wide range of methods college teachers can use to obtain useful feedback on what, how much, and how well their students are learning. Classroom assessment helps instructors to monitor students' learning continuously so that they can identify (and respond with instructional changes to) gaps between what the teacher thinks he or she is teaching and what students are actually learning.

Teachers have an additional important source of feedback, another significant voice to listen to: their own. Because college teachers often have a strong need to seek self-determined competence by continuously scanning the instructional environment for informative feedback, their behavior can be examined—and the source of changes in their behavior understood—by viewing them as "reflective practitioners." Activities that constitute reflective practice or practice-centered inquiry—which have been shown to be useful strategies for instructional improvement—can be arranged along a continuum. At one end are the informal observations, questions, and realizations that arise in the act of teaching, coupled with the immediate reflections on them during and shortly after class. In the middle of the continuum are more persistent, yet still informal, efforts at observation and inquiry (for example, notes taken and records kept). At the other end of the continuum, reflective practice takes place within the framework of a more formal design for research.

The ultimate foundation of all reflective practice or self-reflection is the ability and opportunity to engage in self-evaluation or self-assessment. Two common methods of collecting feedback based on self-evaluation at universities involve the use of self-rating forms and self-reports. At some colleges and universities, for example, faculty are asked to complete the same (or slightly reworded) teaching evaluation questionnaires as their students. This procedure enables faculty to analyze their work and to reflect on their teaching along the same dimensions their students use to evaluate them. A second method, self-reports completed by college professors, has traditionally been limited to vitae and reports of activities; recently, however, the idea of self-reports has been conceptually and functionally expanded into the use of teaching portfolios. These portfolios essentially represent an elaborate and reflective form of self-evaluation. They usually contain the products of good teaching, material from the teachers themselves, and information from others. Unlike most other strategies for improving instruction, these portfolios provide opportunities for professors to reflect on their own teaching within the content of their own disciplines and within the context of their own particular classes; thus, the concept of a teaching portfolio is based squarely on the notion of viewing a teacher as a reflective practitioner.

Although supportive teaching cultures and effective practices of informative feedback from a variety of sources are generally beneficial for the improvement of instruction, specific tailoring might be needed for certain categories of teachers. One such group consists of new and junior faculty. Because new faculty share common concerns about such things as workload and stress from multiple demands, uncertainty about what is expected of them, a desire for collegial support, and a need to develop teaching skills, a strong argument can be made for supplementing traditional, individual approaches of socialization that help them adjust to their new environment with a collective approach that addresses these common concerns. Workshops and what have been called "substantial" orientation programs for new faculty (which offer concrete assistance with the development of teaching skills and consider other matters of importance to new faculty) are being used successfully in a variety of colleges and universities. In addition, formal mentoring programs for new and junior faculty members are also being used at different schools to give concrete assistance with the development of teaching skills, to address various professional and personal concerns, and, in general, to counter the vagaries of the usually informal socialization of new college teachers.

Even the best informative feedback (within the context of the most supportive of teaching cultures) would come to naught if individual teachers ignored it or did not act upon it. What, then, motivates individual teachers to want to improve their teaching and to produce and maintain actual changes in attitudes and behavior? The general theory of change comprising the three stages of unfreezing, changing, and refreezing can be applied here. During unfreezing, the motivation to change is created. A teacher experiences "disconfirmation" cues from his or her environment. Such cues refer to information—including informative feedback from the various sources discussed in this report—indicating that the individual's present attitudes and behaviors are not achieving the goals or producing the kinds of results that would be consistent with his or her current self-image as a teacher. The teacher "compares" information on the outcomes of his or her actual behavior to outcomes that he or she would desire and consider important or ideal. Any incongruence could lead to a sense of anxiety or inadequacy related to not achieving some aspect of one's ideal self-image. A desire to eliminate such disequilibrium might well motivate change (provided that the individual can envision ways to change that will produce results that reestablish his or her positive self-image as a teacher without feeling any loss of integrity or identity).

After the unfreezing stage has produced a motivation to improve one's teaching, the individual searches out new ideas and new information (or considers ideas and information he or she has already received from various sources) to develop new attitudes and behaviors that will be rewarding and confirming (both by the self and others). Any cognitive redefinitions and changes in instructional behaviors and teaching practices are likely to be sustained (refreezing) when the new behaviors and practices are encouraged by others (reconfirmation) and fit into the total personality of the teacher (integration).

Expanding the Scope and Extending the Analytic Framework of This Report

The scope of this report might be expanded and its analytic framework extended in several ways. First, this report has focused primarily on full-time faculty. Yet part-time faculty and teaching assistants (graduate students) do much teaching at our colleges and universities. The material in this report obviously is relevant to these particular teachers, although a fuller report would *explicitly* show how the teaching culture and various sources of informative feedback are of value to them. Although far from common, exemplary programs for helping part-time faculty to develop their professional and pedagogical skills do exist (Gappa 1984; Gappa and Leslie 1993; Millis 1994). Similarly, certain excellent training programs for teaching assistants can be found (Association of American Colleges and Universities and Council of Graduate Schools 1994; Cage 1996; Lambert and Tice 1993; Nyquist, Abbott, and Wulff 1989). The training of teaching assistants is especially valuable because of its double importance—to the quality of undergraduate instruction and to the preparation of future teachers (Richlin 1993).

The model for instructional improvement offered in this report is open to changes in the emphases of its elements. For example, we have taken seriously the importance of academic departments and divisions to the process of improving instruction. Thus, as seen in figure 1 (p. 17), chairs of academic departments are analyzed as an important source of informative feedback for individual instructors, as are a teacher's colleagues (who are likely to be from the teacher's own department). Moreover, academic departments obviously take part in several of the activities identified (in the third section) as particularly supportive to teaching and its improvement—namely, a teaching demonstration or pedagogical colloquium as part of the department's hiring process, collegial interaction and collaboration about teaching, departmental chairs who support a teaching culture, and the connection of rigorous evaluation of teaching to decisions about promotion and tenure. Still, it would be possible to give academic departments and their importance to the improvement of teaching even more prominence in our model. Indeed, it will need to be done if "collaborative departments" (Wergin 1994) become established in universities. These sorts of departments and similar academic units—to a degree not currently seen in most colleges and universities—would be "self-directed *collectives* working cooperatively toward goals [including, presumably, effective teaching] derived from a well-articulated institutional mission . . ." (p. vii). In this vision of "cultures of collective responsibility," an institution's performance incentives and rewards would focus on the departmental "team," and faculty rewards would be based on individual contributions to that team.

The insights and results of certain theoretical and empirical bodies of work might supplement our model. For instance, other general theories of human motivation, thought, and action might add to the general theory of change used here (unfreezing, changing, and refreezing). One possibility is Bandura's social cognitive theory (1986), which "embraces an interactional model of causation in which environmental events, personal factors, and behavior all operate as interacting determinants of each other" (p. xi). Another body of work that might supplement our report is the theoretical and research literature on total quality management or TQM (Sashkin and Kiser 1993) as applied to institutions of higher education (Chizmar 1994; Williams 1993). TQM teaching/learning models have been developed in which the student is perceived as a customer. In these models, the principles of TQM—including continuous improvement, consistent quality, staff/student participation, meeting customers' (i.e., students') needs, coordination, management procedures that detect poor quality and encourage good quality—are seen as contributing to efficient and effective higher education.

Questions of epistemology are not explicitly discussed in this report, although they do lie in the background, and more direct exploration of such questions would be of interest. For example, the third section briefly mentions "a broader definition of scholarship." Various new forms of scholarship (including the scholarship of teaching as well as the scholarship of application and that of integration) could challenge the epistemology built into the modern research university (Schon 1995). These new forms of scholarship "imply a kind of action research with norms of . . . [their] own, which will conflict with the norms of technical rationality—the prevailing epistemology built into the research universities" (p. 27). Thus, if teaching is to be seen as a form of scholarship, "the practice of teaching must be seen as giving rise to new forms of knowledge" (p. 31). Changing universities to incorporate new forms of scholarship would include introducing action research as a legitimate and appropriately rigorous way of knowing and generating knowledge.

Finally, this report has been written within what has been called the "instructional paradigm"—not surprising as most of the work reviewed is grounded in this paradigm. Students' learning is obviously a concern of this approach; consideration of effective instruction, after all, includes consideration of what, and how much, students learn. Yet learning considerations are often not *systematically* emphasized and presented in the instructional paradigm. Many analysts and educators believe that we need to improve pedagogical practice by strengthening the links between teaching and learning: "For too long, our ego involvement in teaching has resulted in benign neglect of learning. It is true that better teaching does frequently produce more and better learning, but a focus on learning is just as likely to make for better teaching. It's not that one is more important than the other. The two are inseparably linked, which we understand in theory but often ignore in practice" (Weimer 1996, pp. 2–3).

"The role of the faculty member involves more than the transfer of information. . . . In this framework, the teacher functions more as a manager who triages and then monitors a variety of instructional tasks that we know are positively associated with learning" (Menges and Weimer 1996, p. 147). Even so, this explanation does not see the role of teacher as completely different from what it is conventionally taken to be:

> *Some of the work in this new paradigm is different. It employs strategies and orientations that are alternatives to the conventional teaching role. But much of the work is the same. Teachers still plan and organize courses. They still design assignments and assess student performance on the assignments. But even these customary instructional tasks are thought about in new ways. What we propose, then, is not more or less work for faculty but work of a different kind—work, we believe, with a clearer sense of focus and purpose. It is teaching considered principally in terms of its impact on students and learning* (Menges and Weimer 1996, pp. 147–48).

Others, however, have called for a more dramatic paradigmatic shift—that is, "focusing on universities upside down: from faculty productivity to student productivity, from faculty disciplinary interests to what students need to learn, from faculty teaching styles to student learning styles, from classroom teaching to student learning" (Guskin 1994, p. 25). Similarly, the mission of our colleges and universities is seen *not* as "instruction but rather that of producing *learning* with every student by *whatever* means work best" (Barr and Tagg 1995, p. 13). Instructional and learning paradigms differ in how they view the teaching/learning theories underlying the activities of higher education, the missions and purposes of colleges and universities, criteria for success of these organizations, their teaching/learning structures, their productivity and funding, and the nature of the roles for college employees (Barr and Tagg 1995). To the extent that colleges and universities adopt the learning paradigm, the model of instructional improvement offered in this report will have to be changed accordingly.

Concluding Comments
This report is about improving teaching, although it is not a presentation of tips or tools for teaching in the college classroom (see, e.g., Davis 1993; McKeachie 1994), as valuable as

such presentations are. Nor is it an examination of the theory and research on teaching and learning (see Feldman and Paulsen 1994). Rather, it reviews pertinent literature on organizational activities, programs, and projects that purport to improve teaching on a campus in order to discover which of them have been shown to be the most consistently effective. It tries to give enough detailed description of the various strategies to be helpful to those setting up programs to improve teaching. And it has tried to go beyond a "menu" of practices—by embedding the various improvement strategies in an analytic or conceptual framework emphasizing supportive teaching cultures that facilitate informative feedback from major sources at a university. In all, a primary purpose of this report is to serve as a stimulator of renewed interest in improving instruction and as a source of guidance, direction, and ideas for deans, department chairs, faculty leaders, and others who want to initiate, expand, or revitalize instructional improvement on campus.

Across universities and colleges, the number of programs for improving instruction has apparently increased over the past 15 years or so. It certainly is true that the *variety* of approaches to improving instruction has increased. Moreover, some new approaches being tried are more venturesome; colleges are experimenting with new strategies to help nurture supportive teaching cultures and to increase the effectiveness of facilitative feedback to teachers.

Well-honed research about instructional improvement is particularly important to the implementation of various programs for improving instruction. Teachers are more likely to change their pedagogical practices when a good research base for doing so is available. Thus, it is of more than routine interest that an admirably wide variety of research methods, including survey research, in-depth interviews, field experiments, ethnographic accounts, and case studies, has been used to gather information about programs and strategies and to evaluate their effectiveness.

Yet certain gaps remain in the available research. For instance, although a fair amount of research exists on the general role of department chairs, research on the ways that chairs can most effectively facilitate the improvement of instruction is only in its early stages. In other areas, moreover, strategies for improving teaching have been claimed to be effective on relatively weak evidence. Indeed, on several

. . . a primary purpose of this report is to serve as a stimulator of renewed interest in improving instruction and as a source of guidance, direction, and ideas . . .

occasions, this report has had to rely on research that might be called "descriptive" or "advocacy" research. This research either did not assess outcomes or did not check systematically on implementation.

On a larger scale, the field has yet to develop a comprehensive conceptual and analytic framework (as well as an organized body of knowledge) for understanding instructional change in terms of settings, processes, strategies, and the like. What will probably prove to be most useful here is the development of an integrative framework laying out the individual, interpersonal, group, and organizational influences on instructional change. While work has begun in this area, much remains to be done.

Although this report is filled with descriptions of effective practices and strategies for improving teaching, we need to know more about how to implement them and to prioritize them. Which practices work best for which faculty? Is it easier to implement these strategies at some schools and harder at others? Does implementation need to be tailored by academic discipline? Does a special "synergy" exist between some of the practices? If the time of teachers, students, and staff, materials, and space are costs, are some strategies or practices more cost-effective than others? In short, which strategies and practices work best under what conditions and at what costs?

More than "good will" is required to implement the programs that have been devised to improve teaching. More needs to be known about the existence and nature of various road blocks and how to remove them or get around them. Each college or university has its own politics and biases, some of which hinder the implementation of activities to improve teaching. More broadly put, the competing cultures, scarce resources, different sets of values about what is important, power differentials, intractable groups and people at today's colleges and universities all affect the implementation and effectiveness of programs.

Teaching will not be improved at our colleges and universities by wishing it so. This report contains both implicit and explicit recommendations for improving instruction in higher education institutions along with specific strategies for their implementation. At this point, it is worth restating the broadest of these recommendations. If colleges are seriously interested in improving their instruction, then ways need to be found to "unfreeze" certain attitudes and behaviors of some teachers that prevent them from improving their teaching. Supportive teaching cultures on campus must be strengthened, especially at those colleges where such cultures are subsidiary to more dominant ones. More teachers need to be given guided experience in being "reflective practitioners." Students should be treated (and sought out) as active partners in the improvement of instruction. Formal as well as informal collaboration among colleagues in the teaching venture should be rewarded. Chairs need to be encouraged to offer the invaluable support they can bring through their creating an environment conducive to effective teaching. Trained consultants—often (though not invariably) associated with campus teaching centers—should be recognized as the experts they are in instructional improvement and their activities facilitated. And new and junior faculty must be encouraged and helped with their teaching through programs recognizing their special needs and talents. The more that colleges "take teaching seriously," the more individual faculty members will too.

REFERENCES

The Educational Resources Information Center (ERIC) Clearinghouse on Higher Education abstracts and indexes the current literature on higher education for inclusion in ERIC's database and
announcement in ERIC's monthly bibliographic journal, *Resources
in Education* (RIE). Most of these publications are available
through the ERIC Document Reproduction Service (EDRS). For
publications cited in this bibliography that are available from EDRS,
ordering number and price code are included. Readers who wish
to order a publication should write to the ERIC Document
Reproduction Service, 3900 Wheeler Avenue, Alexandria, Virginia
22304. (Phone orders with VISA or MasterCard are taken at
800/227-ERIC or 703/823-0500.) When ordering, please specify the
document (ED) number. Documents are available as noted in
microfiche (MF) and paper copy (PC). If you have the price code
ready when you call EDRS, an exact price can be quoted. The last
page of the latest issue of *Resources in Education* also has the
current cost, listed by code.

Abbott, Robert D., Donald H. Wulff, Jody D. Nyquist, Vickie A.
Ropp, and Carla W. Hess. 1990. "Satisfaction with Processes of
Collecting Student Opinions about Instruction: The Student
Perspective." *Journal of Educational Psychology* 82(2): 201–6.

Abbott, Robert D., Donald H. Wulff, and C. Kati Szego. 1989.
"Review of Research on TA Training." In *Teaching Assistant
Training in the 1990s,* edited by Jody D. Nyquist, Robert D.
Abbott, and Donald H. Wulff. New Directions for Teaching and
Learning No. 39. San Francisco: Jossey-Bass.

Adam, Bronwyn E., and Alton O. Roberts. 1993. "Differences
among the Disciplines." In *Recognizing Faculty Work: Reward
Systems for the Year 2000,* edited by Robert M. Diamond and
Bronwyn E. Adam. New Directions for Higher Education No. 81.
San Francisco: Jossey-Bass.

Aitken, Norman D., and Mary Deane Sorcinelli. 1994. "Academic
Leaders and Faculty Developers: Creating an Institutional
Culture that Values Teaching." *To Improve the Academy* 13:
63 –77.

Allaire, Yvan, and Mihaela E. Firsirotu. 1984. "Theories of
Organizational Culture." *Organization Studies* 5(3): 193 –226.

Ambrose, Susan A. 1990. "Faculty Development through Faculty
Luncheon Seminars: A Case Study of Carnegie-Mellon
University." *To Improve the Academy* 9: 123–37.

———. 1995. "Fitting Programs to Institutional Cultures: The

Founding and Evolution of the University Teaching Center." In *Improving College Teaching,* edited by Peter Seldin. Bolton, Mass.: Anker.

Amundsen, Cheryl, Danielle Gryspeerdt, and Katherine Moxness. 1993. "Practice-Centred Inquiry: Developing More Effective Teaching." *Review of Higher Education* 16(3): 329–53.

Anderson, Erin, ed. 1993. *Campus Use of the Teaching Portfolio.* Washington, D.C.: American Association for Higher Education.

Angelo, Thomas A. 1990. "Classroom Assessment: Improving Learning Quality Where It Matters Most." In *The Changing Face of College Teaching,* edited by Marilla D. Svinicki. New Directions for Teaching and Learning No. 42. San Francisco: Jossey-Bass.

———. 1991a. "Introduction and Overview: From Classroom Assessment to Classroom Research." In *Classroom Research: Early Lessons from Success,* edited by Thomas A. Angelo. New Directions for Teaching and Learning No. 46. San Francisco: Jossey-Bass.

———. 1991b. "Ten Easy Pieces: Assessing Higher Learning in Four Dimensions." In *Classroom Research: Early Lessons from Success,* edited by Thomas A. Angelo. New Directions for Teaching and Learning No. 46. San Francisco: Jossey-Bass.

Angelo, Thomas A., and K. Patricia Cross. 1993. *Classroom Assessment Techniques: A Handbook for College Faculty.* San Francisco: Jossey-Bass.

Annis, Linda F. 1989. "Partners in Teaching Improvement." *Journal of Staff, Program and Organization Development* 7(1): 7–13.

Argyris, Chris, Robert Putnam, and Diana McLain Smith. 1985. *Action Science.* San Francisco: Jossey-Bass.

Armour, Robert A. 1995. "Using Campus Culture to Foster Improved Teaching." In *Improving College Teaching,* edited by Peter Seldin. Bolton, Mass.: Anker.

Association of American Colleges. 1985. "Perspectives on Teaching from 'Integrity in the College Curriculum: A Report to the Academic Community.'" *College Teaching* 33(3): 117–24.

Association of American Colleges and Universities and Council of Graduate Schools. 1994. *Preparing Future Faculty: Program Descriptions.* Washington, D.C.: Author.

Austin, Ann E. 1990a. "Faculty Cultures, Faculty Values." In *Assessing Academic Climates and Cultures,* edited by William G. Tierney. New Directions for Institutional Research No. 68. San Francisco: Jossey-Bass.

————. 1990b. *To Leave an Indelible Mark: Encouraging Good Teaching in Research Universities through Faculty Development*. Nashville: Peabody College of Vanderbilt University.

————. 1992. "Supporting Junior Faculty through a Teaching Fellows Program." In *Developing New and Junior Faculty*, edited by Mary Deane Sorcinelli and Ann E. Austin. New Directions for Teaching and Learning No. 50. San Francisco: Jossey-Bass.

Austin, Ann E., and Roger G. Baldwin. 1991. *Faculty Collaboration: Enhancing the Quality of Scholarship and Teaching*. ASHE-ERIC Higher Education Report No. 7. Washington, D.C.: George Washington Univ., School of Education and Human Development. ED 346 805. 138 pp. MF–01; PC–06.

Austin, Ann E., and Zelda E. Gamson. 1983. *Academic Workplace: New Demands, Heightened Tensions*. ASHE-ERIC Higher Education Report No. 10. Washington, D.C.: Association for the Study of Higher Education. ED 243 397. 131 pp. MF–01; PC–06.

Austin, Ann E., and Mary Deane Sorcinelli. 1992. "Summary and Further Reflections." In *Developing New and Junior Faculty*, edited by Mary Deane Sorcinelli and Ann E. Austin. New Directions for Teaching and Learning No. 50. San Francisco: Jossey-Bass.

Baldwin, Roger G. 1979. "Adult and Career Development: What Are the Implications for Faculty?" *Current Issues in Higher Education* 2: 13–20.

————. 1990. "Faculty Career Stages and Implications for Professional Development." In *Enhancing Faculty Careers*, edited by Jack H. Schuster and Daniel W. Wheeler. San Francisco: Jossey-Bass.

Baldwin, Roger G., and Ann E. Austin. 1995. "Faculty Collaboration in Teaching." In *Improving College Teaching*, edited by Peter Seldin. Bolton, Mass.: Anker.

Baldwin, Roger G., and Robert T. Blackburn. 1981. "The Academic Career as a Developmental Process." *Journal of Higher Education* 52(6): 598–614.

Bandura, Albert. 1986. *Social Foundations of Thought and Action: A Social Cognitive Approach*. Englewood Cliffs, N.J.: Prentice-Hall.

Barnett, Marva A. 1983. "Peer Observation and Analysis: Improving Teaching and Training TAs." *ADFL Bulletin* 15(1): 30–33.

Barr, Robert B., and John Tagg. 1995. "From Teaching to Learning: A New Paradigm for Undergraduate Education." *Change* 27(6): 12–25.

Bell, M.E., E.C. Dobson, and J.M. Gram. 1977. "Peer Observation as a Method of Faculty Development." *CUPA Journal* 28(4): 15–17.

Bell, Thomas L., and Tricia McClam. 1992. "Peer Review of Teaching at UTK: An Assessment." ED 350 899. 26 pp. MF–01; PC–02.

Bennett, William E. 1987. "Small-Group Instructional Diagnosis: A Dialogic Approach to Instructional Improvement for Tenured Faculty." *Journal of Staff, Program and Organization Development* 5(3): 100 –104.

Bennett, William J. 1984. *To Reclaim a Legacy.* Washington, D.C.: National Endowment for the Humanities.

Bensimon, Estela M. 1989. "The Meaning of 'Good Presidential Leadership': A Frame Analysis." *Review of Higher Education* 12(2): 107–23.

Bergquist, William H. 1992. *The Four Cultures of the Academy.* San Francisco: Jossey-Bass.

Bergquist, William H., and Steven R. Phillips. 1975. *A Handbook for Faculty Development.* Washington, D.C.: Council for the Advancement of Small Colleges.

———. 1977. *A Handbook for Faculty Development.* Vol. 2. Washington, D.C.: Council for the Advancement of Small Colleges.

Berman, Judith, and Kelley M. Skeff. 1988. "Developing the Motivation for Improving University Teaching." *Innovative Higher Education* 12(2): 114–25.

Bess, James L. 1977. "The Motivation to Teach." *Journal of Higher Education* 48(3): 243–58.

Blackburn, Robert T. 1979. "Academic Careers: Patterns and Possibilities." *Current Issues in Higher Education* 2: 25–28.

———. 1985. "Faculty Career Development: Theory and Practice." In *Faculty Vitality and Institutional Productivity,* edited by Shirley M. Clark and Darrell R. Lewis. New York: Teachers College Press.

Bogotch, Ira E., and Jeanie Bernard. 1994. "A Professor-Coach Relationship in Educational Administration: Learning to Lead." Paper presented at an annual meeting of the American Educational Research Association, April, New Orleans, Louisiana. ED 374 521. 18 pp. MF–01; PC–01.

Boice, Robert. 1984. "Reexamination of Traditional Emphases in Faculty Development." *Research in Higher Education* 21(2): 195–209.

———. 1990. "Mentoring New Faculty: A Program for Implementation." *Journal of Staff, Program and Organization Develop-ment* 8(3): 143–60.

———. 1991a. "New Faculty as Colleagues." *Qualitative Studies in Education* 4(1): 29–44.

———. 1991b. "New Faculty as Teachers." *Journal of Higher Education* 62(2): 150–73.

———. 1991c. "Quick Starters: New Faculty Who Succeed." In *Effective Practices for Improving Teaching,* edited by Michael Theall and Jennifer Franklin. New Directions for Teaching and Learning No. 48. San Francisco: Jossey-Bass.

———. 1992a. "Lessons Learned about Mentoring." In *Developing New and Junior Faculty,* edited by Mary Deane Sorcinelli and Ann E. Austin. New Directions for Teaching and Learning No. 50. San Francisco: Jossey-Bass.

———. 1992b. *The New Faculty Member.* San Francisco: Jossey-Bass.

———. 1993. "New Faculty Involvement for Women and Minorities." *Research in Higher Education* 34(3): 291–341.

Bowen, Howard R., and Jack H. Schuster. 1986. *American Professors: A National Resource Imperiled.* New York: Oxford Univ. Press.

Boyer, Ernest L. 1987. *College: The Undergraduate Experience in America.* New York: Harper & Row.

———. 1990. *Scholarship Reconsidered: Priorities of the Professoriate.* Princeton: Carnegie Foundation for the Advancement of Teaching. ED 326 194. 151 pp. MF–01; PC not available EDRS.

Branch, Virginia. 1995. "Teaching Is 'Job Number One': New Faculty at a Comprehensive University." *Journal of Staff, Program and Organization Development* 12(4): 209–18.

Braskamp, Larry A., Dale C. Brandenburg, and John C. Ory. 1984. *Evaluating Teaching Effectiveness.* Beverly Hills, Cal.: Sage.

Braskamp, Larry A., Deborah L. Fowler, and John C. Ory. 1984. "Faculty Development and Achievement: A Faculty's View." *Review of Higher Education* 7(3): 205–22.

Braskamp, Larry A., and John C. Ory. 1994. *Assessing Faculty Work.* San Francisco: Jossey-Bass.

Brinko, Kathleen T. 1990. "Instructional Consultation with Feedback in Higher Education." *Journal of Higher Education* 61(1): 65–83.

———. 1991. "The Interactions of Teaching Improvement." In *Effective Practices for Improving Teaching,* edited by Michael Theall and Jennifer Franklin. New Directions for Teaching and Learning No. 48. San Francisco: Jossey-Bass.

————. 1993. "The Practice of Giving Feedback to Improve Teaching: What Is Effective?" *Journal of Higher Education* 64(5): 574–93.

Brinko, Kathleen T., and Robert J. Menges, eds. *In press. Practically Speaking: A Sourcebook for Instructional Consultants in Higher Education.* Stillwater, Okla.: New Forums Press.

Brittingham, Barbara E. 1988. "Undergraduate Students' Use of Time: A Classroom Investigation." *To Improve the Academy* 7: 45–52.

Brookfield, Stephen D. 1986. *Understanding and Facilitating Adult Learning.* San Francisco: Jossey-Bass.

————. 1995. *Becoming a Critically Reflective Teacher.* San Francisco: Jossey-Bass.

Brubacher, John A., and Willis Rudy. 1968. *Higher Education in Transition: A History of American Colleges and Universities, 1636–1968.* New York: Harper & Row.

Bushnell, John H. 1962. "Student Culture at Vassar." In *The American College,* edited by Nevitt Sanford. New York: John Wiley & Sons.

Byrnes, Heidi. 1995. "One Department's Experience." *AAHE Bulletin* 47(9): 7+.

Caffarella, Rosemary S. 1993. "Self-Directed Learning." In *An Update on Adult Learning Theory,* edited by Sharan B. Merriam. New Directions for Adult and Continuing Education No. 57. San Francisco: Jossey-Bass.

Cage, Mary Crystal. 20 January 1995. "Regulating Faculty Workloads." *Chronicle of Higher Education* 41(19): A30+.

————. 9 February 1996. "Teaching 101." *Chronicle of Higher Education* 42(22): A19–A20.

Cameron, Kim S., and Deborah R. Ettington. 1988. "The Conceptual Foundations of Organizational Culture." In Vol. 4 of *Higher Education: Handbook of Theory and Research,* edited by John C. Smart. New York: Agathon Press.

Candy, Philip C. 1991. *Self-Direction for Lifelong Learning.* San Francisco: Jossey-Bass.

Carnegie Commission on Higher Education. 1973. *The Purposes and the Performance of Higher Education in the United States.* New York: McGraw-Hill.

Carnegie Foundation for the Advancement of Teaching. 1989. *The Condition of the Professoriate: Attitudes and Trends, 1989.* Princeton, N.J.: Princeton Univ. Press. ED 312 963. 162 pp. MF–01; PC not available EDRS.

Carroll, J. Gregory. 1981. "Faculty Self-Evaluation." In *Handbook of*

Teacher Evaluation, edited by Jason Millman. Beverly Hills, Cal.: Sage.

Carroll, J. Gregory, and Stella R. Goldberg. 1989. "Teaching Consultants: A Collegial Approach to Better Teaching." *College Teaching* 37(4): 143 –54.

Cash, William B., and Robert L. Minter. 1979. "Consulting Approaches: Two Basic Styles." *Training and Development Journal* 33(9): 26 –28.

Cashin, William E. 1989. "Defining and Evaluating College Teaching." IDEA Paper No. 21. Manhattan: Kansas State Univ., Center for Faculty Evaluation and Development. ED 339 731. 6 pp. MF–01; PC–01.

Centra, John A. 1972. *Strategies for Improving College Teaching.* Higher Education Report No 8. Washington, D.C.: American Association for Higher Education. ED 071 616. 53 pp. MF–01; PC–03.

———. 1973a. "Effectiveness of Student Feedback in Modifying College Instruction." *Journal of Educational Psychology* 65(3): 395–401.

———. 1973b. "Self-Ratings of College Teachers: A Comparison with Student Ratings." *Journal of Educational Measurement* 10(4): 287–95.

———. 1975. "Colleagues as Raters of Classroom Instruction." *Journal of Higher Education* 46(1): 327–35.

———. 1979. *Determining Faculty Effectiveness.* San Francisco: Jossey-Bass.

———. 1993. *Reflective Faculty Evaluation.* San Francisco: Jossey-Bass.

Centra, John A., Robert C. Froh, Peter J. Gray, and Leo M. Lambert. 1987. *A Guide to Evaluating Teaching for Promotion and Tenure.* Acton, Mass.: Copley.

Cerbin, William. 1994. "The Course Portfolio as a Tool for Continuous Improvement of Teaching and Learning." *Journal on Excellence in College Teaching* 5(1): 95–105.

Chaffee, Ellen E., and William G. Tierney. 1988. *Collegiate Culture and Leadership Strategy.* New York: ACE/Macmillan.

Chism, Nancy V., and Donald P. Sanders. 1986. "The Place of Practice-Centered Inquiry in a Faculty Development Program." *To Improve the Academy* 5: 56–64.

Chism, Nancy, Donald Sanders, and Connie Zitlow. 1987. "Observations on a Faculty Development Program Based on Practice-Centered Inquiry." *Peabody Journal of Education* 65(1): 1–23.

Chizmar, John F. 1994. "Total Quality Management (TQM) of Teaching and Learning." *Journal of Economic Education* 25(2): 179–90.

Clark, Burton R. 1970. *The Distinctive College: Reed, Antioch, and Swarthmore.* Chicago: Aldine.

———. 1972. "The Organizational Saga in Higher Education." *Administrative Science Quarterly* 17(2): 178–84.

———. 1985. "Listening to the Professoriate." *Change* 17(5): 36–43.

———. 1987a. *The Academic Life: Small Worlds, Different Worlds.* Princeton, N.J.: Carnegie Foundation for the Advancement of Teaching. ED 299 902. 376 pp. MF– 01; PC not available EDRS.

———. 1987b. *The Academic Profession: National, Disciplinary, and Institutional Settings.* Berkeley: Univ. of California Press.

Clark, Burton R., and Martin Trow. 1966. "The Organizational Context." In *College Peer Groups,* edited by Theodore M. Newcomb and E.K. Wilson. Chicago: Aldine.

Clark, D. Joseph, and Jean Bekey. 1979. "Use of Small Groups in Instructional Evaluation." *POD Quarterly* 1(2): 87–95.

Clark, M. Carolyn. 1993. "Transformational Learning." In *An Update on Adult Learning Theory,* edited by Sharan B. Merriam. New Directions for Adult and Continuing Education No. 57. San Francisco: Jossey-Bass.

Coffman, Sara Jane. 1991. "Improving Your Teaching through Small-Group Diagnosis." *College Teaching* 39(2): 80–82.

Cohen, Peter A. 1980. "Effectiveness of Student-Rating Feedback for Improving College Instruction: A Meta-analysis of Findings." *Research in Higher Education* 13(4): 321–41.

Cohen, Peter A., and Wilbert J. McKeachie. 1980. "The Role of Colleagues in the Evaluation of College Teaching." *Improving College and University Teaching* 28(4): 147–54.

Cooper, Colleen R. 1982. "Getting Inside the Instructional Process: A Collaborative Diagnostic Process for Improving College Teaching." *Journal of Instructional Development* 5(3): 2–10.

Cottell, Philip G. 1991. "Classroom Research in Accounting: Assessing for Learning." In *Classroom Research: Early Lessons from Success,* edited by Thomas A. Angelo. New Directions for Teaching and Learning No. 46. San Francisco: Jossey-Bass.

Cowley, W.H. 1958. "College and University Teaching, 1858–1958." In *The Two Ends of the Log: Learning and Teaching in Today's College,* edited by R.M. Cooper. Minneapolis: Univ. of Minnesota Press.

Cox, Milton D. 1994. "Reclaiming Teaching Excellence: Miami

University's Teaching Scholars Program." *To Improve the Academy* 13: 79–96.

———. 1995. "The Development of New and Junior Faculty." In *Teaching Improvement Practices,* edited by W. Alan Wright. Bolton, Mass.: Anker.

Cranton, Patricia. 1994. "Self-Directed and Transformative Instructional Development." *Journal of Higher Education* 65(6): 726–44.

Creswell, John W., Daniel W. Wheeler, Alan T. Seagren, Nancy J. Egly, and Kirk D. Beyer. 1990. *The Academic Chairperson's Handbook.* Lincoln: Univ. of Nebraska Press.

Cross, K. Patricia. 1986. "A Proposal to Improve Teaching, or What 'Taking Teaching Seriously' Should Mean." *AAHE Bulletin* 38(1): 9–14.

Cross, K. Patricia, and Thomas A. Angelo. 1988. *Classroom Assessment Techniques.* Ann Arbor, Mich.: National Center for Research to Improve Postsecondary Teaching and Learning.

Cutten, G.B. 25 October 1958. "The College Professor as Teacher." *School and Society* 86: 372–75.

Cytrynbaum, Soloman, Susan Lee, and David Wadner. 1982. "Faculty Development through the Life Course." *Journal of Instructional Development* 5(3): 11–22.

Dahlin, Amber. 1994. "The Teacher as a Reflective Professional." *College Teaching* 42(2): 57–61.

Dalgaard, Kathleen A. 1982. "Some Effects of Training on Teaching Effectiveness of Untrained University Teaching Assistants." *Research in Higher Education* 17(1): 39–50.

Dalgaard, Kathleen A., Deborah E. Simpson, and Carol A. Carrier. 1982. "Coordinate Status Consultation." *Journal of Instructional Development* 5(4): 7–14.

Davis, Barbara Gross. 1993. *Tools for Teaching.* San Francisco: Jossey-Bass.

Deal, Terrence E., and Allan A. Kennedy. 1982. *Corporate Cultures.* Reading, Mass.: Addison-Wesley.

Deci, Edward L., and Richard M. Ryan. 1982. "Intrinsic Motivation to Teach: Possibilities and Obstacles in Our Colleges and Universities." In *Motivating Professors to Teach Effectively,* edited by James L. Bess. New Directions for Teaching and Learning No. 10. San Francisco: Jossey-Bass.

———. 1985. *Intrinsic Motivation and Self-Determination in Human Behavior.* New York: Plenum Press.

Dey, Eric L., Claudia E. Ramirez, William S. Korn, and Alexander

W. Astin. 1993. *The American College Teacher: National Norms for the 1992–93 HERI Survey.* Los Angeles: UCLA, Higher Education Research Institute.

Diamond, Nancy A. 1988. "S.G.I.D. (Small Group Instructional Diagnosis): Tapping Student Perceptions of Teaching." In *A Handbook for Practitioners,* edited by Emily C. Wadsworth. Professional and Organizational Development Network in Higher Education.

Diamond, Robert M. 11 May 1994. "The Tough Task of Reforming the Faculty-Rewards System." *Chronicle of Higher Education:* B1–B3.

Diamond, Robert M., and Bronwyn E. Adam, eds. 1993. *Recognizing Faculty Work: Reward Systems for the Year 2000.* New Directions for Higher Education No. 81. San Francisco: Jossey-Bass.

———, eds. 1995. *The Disciplines Speak: Rewarding the Scholarly, Professional, and Creative Work of Faculty.* Washington, D.C.: American Association for Higher Education.

Diehl, Paul F., and Ronald D. Simpson. 1989. "Investing in Junior Faculty: The Teaching Improvement Program (TIPs)." *Innovative Higher Education* 13(2): 147–57.

Dill, David D. 1982. "The Management of Academic Culture: Notes on the Management of Meaning and Social Integration." *Higher Education* 11(3): 303–20.

DiLorenzo, Thomas M., and P. Paul Heppner. 1994. "The Role of an Academic Department in Promoting Faculty Development: Recognizing Diversity and Leading to Excellence." *Journal of Counseling and Development* 72(5): 485–91.

Dunn, Dana, Linda Rouse, and Monica A. Seff. 1994. "New Faculty Socialization in the Academic Workplace." In Vol. 10 of *Higher Education: Handbook of Theory and Research,* edited by John C. Smart. New York: Agathon Press.

Easterby-Smith, Mark, and Nils-Goran Olve. 1984. "Team Teaching: Making Management Education More Student-Centered?" *Management Education and Development* 15(3): 221–36.

Eble, Kenneth E., and Wilbert J. McKeachie. 1985. *Improving Undergraduate Education through Faculty Development.* San Francisco: Jossey-Bass.

Edgerton, Russell. 1993. "The Reexamination of Faculty Priorities." *Change* 25(4): 10–25.

Edgerton, Russell, Patricia Hutchings, and Kathleen Quinlan. 1991. *The Teaching Portfolio: Capturing the Scholarship in Teaching.*

Washington, D.C.: American Association for Higher Education. ED 353 892. 62 pp. MF–01; PC not available EDRS.

Eison, James A. 1989. "Mandatory Teaching Effectiveness Workshops for New Faculty: What a Difference Three Years Make." *Journal of Staff, Program and Organization Development* 7(2): 59–66.

Eison, James A., and H. Hamner Hill. 1990. "Creating Workshops for New Faculty." *Journal of Staff, Program and Organization Development* 8(4): 223–34.

Eison, James A., and Ellen Stevens. 1995. "Faculty Development Workshops and Institutes." In *Teaching Improvement Practices,* edited by W. Alan Wright. Bolton, Mass.: Anker.

Erickson, Glenn R. 1986. "A Survey of Faculty Development Practices." *To Improve the Academy* 5: 182–96.

———, ed. 1992. *Program Descriptions: A Collection of Brief Descriptions of Faculty, Instructional, and Organizational Development Programs in Higher Education.* Professional and Organizational Development Network in Higher Education.

Erickson, Glenn R., and Bette L. Erickson. 1979. "Improving College Teaching: An Evaluation of a Teaching Consultation Procedure." *Journal of Higher Education* 50(5): 670–83.

Fairweather, James S. 1993. *Teaching, Research, and Faculty Rewards.* University Park: Pennsylvania State Univ., National Center on Postsecondary Teaching, Learning, and Assessment.

Fairweather, James S., and Robert A. Rhoads. 1995. "Teaching and the Faculty Role: Enhancing the Commitment to Instruction in American Colleges and Universities." *Educational Evaluation and Policy Analysis* 17(2): 179–94.

Feldman, Kenneth A. 1976. "Grades and College Students' Evaluations of Their Courses and Teachers." *Research in Higher Education* 4(1): 69–111.

———. 1977. "Consistency and Variability among College Students in Rating Their Teachers and Courses: A Review and Analysis." *Research in Higher Education* 6(3): 223–74.

———. 1978. "Course Characteristics and College Students' Ratings of Their Teachers: What We Know and What We Don't." *Research in Higher Education* 9(3): 199–242.

———. 1983. "Seniority and Experience of College Teachers as Related to Evaluations They Receive from Students." *Research in Higher Education* 18(1): 3–124.

———. 1984. "Class Size and College Students' Evaluations of Teachers and Courses: A Closer Look." *Research in Higher Education* 21(1): 45–116.

————. 1987. "Research Productivity and Scholarly Accomplishment of College Teachers as Related to Their Instructional Effectiveness: A Review and Exploration." *Research in Higher Education* 26(3): 227–91.

————. 1988. "Effective College Teaching from the Students' and Faculty's View: Matched or Mismatched Priorities?" *Research in Higher Education* 28(4): 291–344.

————. 1989. "Instructional Effectiveness of College Teachers as Judged by Teachers Themselves, Current and Former Students, Colleagues, Administrators, and External (Neutral) Observers." *Research in Higher Education* 30(2): 137–94.

————, ed. 1972. *College and Student: Selected Readings in the Social Psychology of Higher Education.* New York: Pergamon Press.

Feldman, Kenneth A., and Theodore M. Newcomb. 1969. *The Impact of College on Students.* San Francisco: Jossey-Bass.

Feldman, Kenneth A., and Michael B. Paulsen, eds. 1994. *Teaching and Learning in the College Classroom.* Needham Heights, Mass.: Ginn Press.

Fenton, Edwin. 1991. "Developing a Culture of Teaching in a Small Research University." Mimeographed. Pittsburgh: Carnegie-Mellon Univ., University Teaching Center.

Ferren, Ann S. 1989. "Faculty Development Can Change the Culture of a College." *To Improve the Academy* 8: 101–16.

Ferren, Ann, and William Geller. 1983. "Classroom Consultants: Colleagues Helping Colleagues." *Improving College and University Teaching* 31(2): 82–86.

Fink, L. Dee. 1992. "Orientation Programs for New Faculty." In *Developing New and Junior Faculty,* edited by Mary Deane Sorcinelli and Ann E. Austin. New Directions for Teaching and Learning No. 50. San Francisco: Jossey-Bass.

————. 1995. "Evaluating Your Own Teaching." In *Improving College Teaching,* edited by Peter Seldin. Bolton, Mass.: Anker.

————, ed. 1984. *The First year of College Teaching.* New Directions for Teaching and Learning No. 17. San Francisco: Jossey-Bass.

Finkelstein, Martin J., and Mark W. LaCelle-Peterson. 1992. "New and Junior Faculty: A Review of the Literature." In *Developing New and Junior Faculty,* edited by Mary Deane Sorcinelli and Ann E. Austin. New Directions for Teaching and Learning No. 50. San Francisco: Jossey-Bass.

Fox, Dennis. 1983. "Personal Theories of Teaching." *Studies in Higher Education* 8(2): 151– 63.

French, Nancy K., and Deanna J. Sands. 1993. "Improving Our Teaching: A Peer Coaching Model." *Issues and Inquiry in College Learning and Teaching* 16(2): 33–56.

French-Lazovik, Grace. 1981. "Peer Review: Documentary Evidence in the Evaluation of Teaching." In *Handbook of Teacher Evaluation,* edited by Jason Millman. Beverly Hills, Cal.: Sage.

Froh, Robert C., Robert J. Menges, and Charles J. Walker. 1993. "Revitalizing Faculty Work through Intrinsic Rewards." In *Recognizing Faculty Work: Reward Systems for the Year 2000,* edited by Robert M. Diamond and Bronwyn E. Adam. New Directions for Higher Education No. 81. San Francisco: Jossey-Bass.

Fuchs, Gordon E., and Louise P. Moore. 1988. "Collaboration for Understanding and Effectiveness." *Clearing House* 61(9): 410–13.

Fuhrmann, Barbara Schneider, and Anthony F. Grasha. 1983. *A Practical Handbook for College Teachers.* Boston: Little, Brown.

Fuller, Frances F., and Brad A. Manning. 1973. "Self-Confrontation Reviewed: A Conceptualization for Video Playback in Teacher Education." *Review of Educational Research* 43(4): 469–528.

Furniss, W. Todd. 1981. *Reshaping Faculty Careers.* Washington, D.C.: American Council on Education.

Gappa, Judith M. 1984. *Part-time Faculty: Higher Education at the Crossroads.* ASHE-ERIC Higher Education Report No. 3. Washington, D.C.: Association for the Study of Higher Education. ED 251 058. 129 pp. MF–01; PC–06.

Gappa, Judith M., and David W. Leslie. 1993. *The Invisible Faculty: Improving the Status of Part-timers in Higher Education.* San Francisco: Jossey-Bass.

Geis, George L. 1991. "The Moment of Truth: Feeding Back Information about Teaching." In *Effective Practices for Improving Teaching,* edited by Michael Theall and Jennifer Franklin. New Directions for Teaching and Learning No. 48. San Francisco: Jossey-Bass.

Gil, Doron H. 1987. "Instructional Evaluation as a Feedback Process." In *Techniques for Evaluating and Improving Instruction,* edited by Lawrence M. Aleamoni. New Directions for Teaching and Learning No. 31. San Francisco: Jossey-Bass.

Gmelch, Walter H. 1995. "The Department Chair's Role in Improving Teaching." In *Improving College Teaching,* edited by Peter Seldin. Bolton, Mass.: Anker.

Gmelch, Walter H., and V.D. Miskin. 1993. *Leadership Skills for Department Chairs.* Bolton, Mass.: Anker.

Golin, Steve. 1990. "Four Arguments for Peer Collaboration and Student Interviewing." *AAHE Bulletin* 43(4): 9–10.

Gray, Peter J., Robert C. Froh, and Robert M. Diamond. 1992. "A National Study of Research Universities: On the Balance between Research and Undergraduate Teaching." Syracuse, N.Y.: Syracuse Univ., Center for Instructional Development. ED 350 967. 23 pp. MF–01; PC–01.

Gregory, Kathleen L. 1983. "Native-View Paradigms: Multiple Cultures and Culture Conflicts in Organizations." *Administrative Science Quarterly* 28(3): 359–76.

Guskin, Alan E. 1994. "Reducing Student Costs and Enhancing Student Learning." *Change* 26(4): 22–29.

Hackman, J. Richard, and Greg R. Oldham. 1976. "Motivation through the Design of Work: Test of a Theory." *Organizational Behavior and Human Performance* 16(2): 250–79.

Halstead, D. Kent. 1989. *Higher Education Tuition.* Washington, D.C.: Research Associates of Washington.

———. 1992. *State Profiles: Financing Public Higher Education.* Washington, D.C.: Research Associates of Washington.

Harcharik, Kathleen Kish. 1994. "Collegial Coaching: Ideas on How to Improve the Process." *Issues and Inquiry in College Learning and Teaching* 17/18(1): 66–79.

Hatch, Mary Jo. 1993. "The Dynamics of Organizational Culture." *Academy of Management Review* 18(4): 657–93.

Hauptman, Arthur M. 1990. *The College Tuition Spiral.* Washington, D.C.: College Board and American Council on Education.

Hawkins, Hugh. 1979. "University Identity: The Teaching and Research Functions." In *The Organization of Knowledge in Modern America, 1860–1920,* edited by Alexandra Oleson and John Voss. Baltimore: Johns Hopkins Univ. Press.

Heath, David A., Nancy Carlson, and Daniel Kurtz. 1987. "Team Teaching Optometry." *Journal of Optometric Education* 12(3): 76–80.

Helling, Barbara B. 1988. "Looking for Good Teaching: A Guide to Peer Observation." *Journal of Staff, Program and Organization Development* 6(4): 147–58.

Helling, Barbara, and Diane Kuhlmann. 1988. "The Faculty Visitor Program: Helping Faculty See Themselves." In *Face to Face: A Sourcebook of Individual Consultation Techniques for Faculty Development Personnel,* edited by Karron G. Lewis and Joyce T. Povlacs. Stillwater, Okla.: New Forums Press.

Hendricson, William D., David W. Hawkins, John H. Littlefield, John H. Kleffner, Nancy C. Hudepohl, and Robert Herbert. 1983. "Effects of Providing Feedback to Lecturers via Videotape

Recordings and Observer Critiques." *American Journal of Pharmaceutical Education* 47(3): 239–44.

Heppner, P. Paul, and Joseph A. Johnston. 1994. "Peer Consultation: Faculty and Students Working Together to Improve Teaching." *Journal of Counseling and Development* 72(5): 492–99.

Hilsen, Linda, and LeAne Rutherford. 1991. "Front-Line Faculty Development: Chairs Constructively Critiquing Colleagues in the Classroom." *To Improve the Academy* 10: 251–69.

Hines, Edward R. 1988. *Higher Education and State Governments: Renewed Partnership, Cooperation, or Competition?* ASHE-ERIC Higher Education Report No. 5. Washington, D.C.: Association for the Study of Higher Education. ED 306 840. 177 pp. MF–01; PC–08.

Hodgkinson, Harold L. 1974. "Adult Development: Implications for Faculty and Administrators." *Educational Record* 55(4): 263 –74.

Holmes, Wendy. 1988. "Art Essays and Computer Letters." *To Improve the Academy* 7: 23–32.

Hughes, Everett, Howard Becker, and Blanche Geer. 1962. "Student Culture and Academic Effort." In *The American College,* edited by Nevitt Sanford. New York: John Wiley & Sons.

Hutchings, Patricia. 1993a. "Introduction." In *Campus Use of the Teaching Portfolio,* edited by Erin Anderson. Washington, D.C.: American Association for Higher Education.

———. 1993b. "Lessons from AAHE's Teaching Initiative." In *Faculty as Teachers,* edited by Maryellen Weimer. University Park: Pennsylvania State Univ., National Center on Postsecondary Teaching, Learning, and Assessment.

Jackson, William K., and Ronald D. Simpson. 1994. "Mentoring New Faculty for Teaching and Research." In *Mentoring Revisited: Making an Impact on Individuals and Institutions,* edited by Marie A. Wunsch. New Directions for Teaching and Learning No. 57. San Francisco: Jossey-Bass.

Jakoubek, Jane. 1994. "A Low-Cost and High-Impact Model for Development and Support of New Faculty." *Journal of Staff, Program and Organization Development* 11(4): 225–33.

Jarvis, Donald K. 1991. *Junior Faculty Development: A Handbook.* New York: Modern Language Association of America.

Jelinek, Mariann, Linda Smircich, and Paul Hirsch. 1983. "Introduction: A Code of Many Colors." *Administrative Science Quarterly* 28(3): 331–38.

Jenrette, Mardee S., and Vince Napoli. 1994. *The Teaching-

Learning Enterprise: Miami-Dade Community College's Blue-print for Change. Bolton, Mass.: Anker.

Johnstone, D. Bruce. 1993. "Enhancing the Productivity of Learning." *AAHE Bulletin* 46(4): 3–5.

Joyce, Bruce, and Beverly Showers. 1982. "The Coaching of Teaching." *Educational Leadership* 40(1): 4–10.

Kahn, Susan. 1993. "Better Teaching through Better Evaluation: A Guide for Faculty and Institutions." *To Improve the Academy* 12: 111–26.

Katz, Joseph, and Mildred Henry. 1988. *Turning Professors into Teachers: A New Approach to Faculty Development and Student Learning.* New York: Macmillan.

Keig, Larry, and Michael D. Waggoner. 1994. *Collaborative Peer Review: The Role of Faculty in Improving College Teaching.* ASHE-ERIC Higher Education Report No. 2. Washington, D.C.: George Washington Univ., School of Education and Human Development. ED 378 925. 193 pp. MF–01; PC–08.

Kerwin, Michael A. 1985. "The Teaching Improvement Process." *Journal of Staff, Program and Organization Development* 3(1): 10–15.

Kerwin, Michael A., and Judith Rhoads. 1993. "The Teaching Consultants' Workshop." *To Improve the Academy* 12: 69–77.

Kilmann, Ralph H., Mary J. Saxton, Roy Serpa, and Associates, eds. 1985. *Gaining Control of the Corporate Culture.* San Francisco: Jossey-Bass.

Kinsella, Kate. 1995. "Peers Coaching Teaching: Colleagues Supporting Professional Growth across the Disciplines." *To Improve the Academy* 14: 107–23.

Kogut, Leonard S. 1984. "Quality Circles: A Japanese Management Technique for the Classroom." *Improving College and University Teaching* 32(3): 123–27.

Kort, Melissa Sue. 1991. "Re-Visioning Our Teaching: Classroom Research and Composition." In *Classroom Research: Early Lessons from Success,* edited by Thomas A. Angelo. New Directions for Teaching and Learning No. 46. San Francisco: Jossey-Bass.

Kuh, George D., and Elizabeth J. Whitt. 1988. *The Invisible Tapestry: Culture in American Colleges and Universities.* ASHE-ERIC Higher Education Report No. 1. Washington, D.C.: Association for the Study of Higher Education. ED 299 934. 160 pp. MF–01; PC–07.

Kurfiss, Joanne G., and Robert Boice. 1990. "Current and Desired

Faculty Development Practices among POD Members." *To Improve the Academy* 9: 73–82.

Kyger, Betty L. 1984. "Using a Class Interview as a Formative Evaluation Technique." *Journal of Staff, Program and Organization Development* 2(4): 97–99.

LaCelle-Peterson, Mark W., and Martin J. Finkelstein. 1993. "Institutions Matter: Campus Teaching Environments' Impact on Senior Faculty." In *Developing Senior Faculty as Teachers,* edited by Martin J. Finkelstein and Mark W. LaCelle-Peterson. New Directions for Teaching and Learning No. 55. San Francisco: Jossey-Bass.

Lambert, Leo M., and Stacey L. Tice, eds. 1993. *Preparing Graduate Students to Teach.* Washington, D.C.: American Association for Higher Education.

Leary, L. 26 September 1959. "The Scholar as Teacher." *School and Society* 87: 362–63.

Levinson, Daniel J. 1986. "A Conception of Adult Development." *American Psychologist* 41(1): 3–13.

Levinson-Rose, Judith, and Robert J. Menges. 1981. "Improving College Teaching: A Critical Review of Research." *Review of Educational Research* 51(3): 403–34.

Lewin, Kurt. 1947. "Group Decision and Social Change." In *Readings in Social Psychology,* edited by T.N. Newcomb and E.L. Hartley. Troy, Mo.: Holt, Rinehart & Winston.

Lewis, Karron G. 1988. "Individual Consultation: Its Importance to Faculty Development Programs." In *Face to Face: A Sourcebook of Individual Consultation Techniques for Faculty Development Personnel,* edited by Karron G. Lewis and Joyce T. Povlacs. Stillwater, Okla.: New Forums Press.

Lewis, Karron G., and Joyce T. Povlacs, eds. 1988. *Face to Face: A Sourcebook of Individual Consultation Techniques for Faculty Development Personnel.* Stillwater, Okla.: New Forums Press.

Lewis, Karron G., Marilla D. Svinicki, and James E. Stice. 1985. "Filling the Gap: Introducing New Faculty to the Basics of Teaching." *Journal of Staff, Program and Organization Development* 3(1): 16–21.

L'Hommedieu, Randi, Robert J. Menges, and Kathleen T. Brinko. 1990. "Methodological Explanations for the Modest Effects of Feedback from Student Ratings." *Journal of Educational Psychology* 82(2): 232–41.

Lord, Blair. 1988. "Student Styles and Learning in Two College of Business Courses." *To Improve the Academy* 7: 57– 62.

Louis, Meryl Reis. 1992. "Organizations as Culture-Bearing Milieux." In *Classics of Organization Theory,* edited by Jay M. Shafritz and J. Steven Ott. Belmont, Cal.: Wadsworth.

Lucas, Ann F. 1990. "The Department Chair as Change Agent." In *How Administrators Can Improve Teaching,* edited by Peter Seldin. San Francisco: Jossey-Bass.

———. 1994. *Strengthening Departmental Leadership.* San Francisco: Jossey-Bass.

———, ed. 1989. *The Department Chairperson's Role in Enhancing College Teaching.* New Directions for Teaching and Learning No. 37. San Francisco: Jossey-Bass.

Lynton, Ernest A., and Sandra E. Elman. 1987. *New Priorities for the University.* San Francisco: Jossey-Bass.

McDaniel, Elizabeth A. 1987. "Faculty Collaboration for Better Teaching: Adult Learning Principles Applied to Teaching Improvement." *To Improve the Academy* 6: 94–102.

McKeachie, Wilbert J. 1979. "Perspectives from Psychology: Financial Incentives Are Ineffective for Faculty." In *Academic Rewards in Higher Education,* edited by Darrell R. Lewis and William E. Becker, Jr. Cambridge, Mass.: Ballinger.

———. 1982. "The Rewards of Teaching." In *Motivating Professors to Teach Effectively,* edited by James L. Bess. New Directions for Teaching and Learning No. 10. San Francisco: Jossey-Bass.

———. 1987. "Can Evaluating Instruction Improve Teaching?" In *Techniques for Evaluating and Improving Teaching,* edited by Lawrence M. Aleamoni. New Directions for Teaching and Learning No. 31. San Francisco: Jossey-Bass.

———. 1994. *Teaching Tips: Strategies, Research, and Theory for College and University Teachers.* Lexington, Mass.: D.C. Heath.

Marsh, Herbert W. 1984. "Students' Evaluations of University Teaching: Dimensionality, Reliability, Validity, Potential Biases, and Utility." *Journal of Educational Psychology* 76(5): 707–54.

———. 1987. "Students' Evaluations of University Teaching: Research Findings, Methodological Issues, and Directions for Future Research." *International Journal of Educational Research* 11(3): 253–388.

Marsh, Herbert W., and Michael J. Dunkin. 1992. "Students' Evaluations of University Teaching: A Multidimensional Perspective." In Vol. 8 of *Higher Education: Handbook of Theory and Research,* edited by John C. Smart. New York: Agathon Press.

Marsh, Herbert W., and Lawrence Roche. 1993. "The Use of Students' Evaluations and an Individually Structured Intervention to

Enhance University Teaching Effectiveness." *American Educational Research Journal* 30(1): 217–51.

Martin, Joanne, and Caren Siehl. Autumn 1983. "Organizational Culture and Counterculture: An Uneasy Symbiosis." *Organizational Dynamics:* 52–64.

Masland, Andrew T. 1985. "Organizational Culture in the Study of Higher Education." *Review of Higher Education* 8(2): 157–68.

Massy, William F., Andrea K. Wilger, and Carol Colbeck. 1994. "Overcoming 'Hollowed' Collegiality." *Change* 26(4): 11–20.

Mathis, B. Claude. 1979. "Academic Careers and Adult Development: A Nexus for Research." *Current Issues in Higher Education* 2: 21–24.

Matoney, Joseph. 1988. "Weekly Quizzes and Examination Performance in Intermediate Accounting." *To Improve the Academy* 7: 53–56.

Menges, Robert J. 1985. "Career-Span Faculty Development." *College Teaching* 33(4): 181–84.

———. 1987. "Colleagues as Catalysts for Change in Teaching." *To Improve the Academy* 6: 83–93.

———. 1991. "The Real World of Teaching Improvement: A Faculty Perspective." In *Effective Practices for Improving Teaching,* edited by Michael Theall and Jennifer Franklin. New Directions for Teaching and Learning No. 48. San Francisco: Jossey-Bass.

———. 1994. "Preparing New Faculty for the Future." *Thought & Action* 10(2): 81–95.

Menges, Robert J., and Kathleen T. Brinko. 1986. "Effects of Student Evaluation Feedback: A Meta-analysis of Higher Education Research." Paper presented at a meeting of the American Educational Research Association, San Francisco, California. ED 270 408. 18 pp. MF–01; PC–01.

Menges, Robert J., and William C. Rando. 1989. "What Are Your Assumptions? Improving Instruction by Examining Theories." *College Teaching* 37(2): 54–60.

Menges, Robert J., and Maryellen Weimer, eds. 1996. *Teaching on Solid Ground: Using Scholarship to Improve Practice.* San Francisco: Jossey-Bass.

Merriam, Sharan B., ed. 1993. *An Update on Adult Learning Theory.* New Directions for Adult and Continuing Education No. 57. San Francisco: Jossey-Bass.

Metzger, Walter P. 1961. *Academic Freedom in the Age of the University.* New York: Columbia Univ. Press.

Mezirow, Jack. 1991. *Transformative Dimensions of Adult Learning.* San Francisco: Jossey-Bass.

Millis, Barbara J. 1989. "Colleagues Helping Colleagues: A Peer Observation Program Model." *Journal of Staff, Program and Organization Development* 7(1): 15–21.

———. 1992. "Conducting Effective Peer Classroom Observations." *To Improve the Academy* 11: 189–206.

———. 1994. "Forging the Ties That Bind: Peer Mentoring Part-time Faculty." In *Mentoring Revisited: Making an Impact on Individuals and Institutions,* edited by Marie A. Wunsch. New Directions for Teaching and Learning No. 57. San Francisco: Jossey-Bass.

Millis, Barbara J., and Barbara B. Kaplan. 1995. "Enhancing Teaching through Peer Classroom Observations." In *Improving College Teaching,* edited by Peter Seldin. Bolton, Mass.: Anker.

Minor, James F., and Kenneth M. Preston. 1991. "Peer Coaching at the Junior College Level: Developing a Nonthreatening Environment." Paper presented at the National Conference on the Adult Learner, Columbia, South Carolina. ED 339 410. 21 pp. MF–01; PC–01.

Murray, Harry G. 1983. "Low-Inference Classroom Teaching Behaviors and Student Ratings of College Teaching Effectiveness." *Journal of Educational Psychology* 75(1): 138–49.

———. 1984. "The Impact of Formative and Summative Evaluation of Teaching in North American Universities." *Assessment and Evaluation in Higher Education* 9(2): 117–32.

———. 1985. "Classroom Teaching Behaviors Related to College Teaching Effectiveness." In *Using Research to Improve Teaching,* edited by Janet G. Donald and Arthur M. Sullivan. New Directions for Teaching and Learning No. 23. San Francisco: Jossey-Bass.

———. 1987a. "Acquiring Student Feedback that Improves Instruction." In *Teaching Large Classes Well,* edited by Maryellen G. Weimer. New Directions for Teaching and Learning No. 32. San Francisco: Jossey-Bass.

———. 1987b. "Impact of Student Instructional Ratings on Quality of Teaching in Higher Education." Paper presented at an annual meeting of the American Educational Research Association, April, Washington, D.C. ED 284 495. 20 pp. MF–01; PC–01.

———. 1991. "Effective Teaching Behaviors in the College Classroom." In Vol. 7 of *Higher Education: Handbook of Theory and Research,* edited by John C. Smart. New York: Agathon Press.

Nakaji, David M. 1991. "Classroom Research in Physics: Gaining

Insights into Visualization and Problem Solving." In *Classroom Research: Early Lessons from Success,* edited by Thomas A. Angelo. New Directions for Teaching and Learning No. 46. San Francisco: Jossey-Bass.

National Institute of Education. 1984. *Involvement in Learning: Realizing the Potential of American Higher Education.* Washington, D.C.: U.S. Government Printing Office.

Nyquist, Jody D., Robert D. Abbott, and Donald H. Wulff, eds. 1989. *Teaching Assistant Training in the 1990s.* New Directions for Teaching and Learning No. 39. San Francisco: Jossey-Bass.

Olsen, Deborah. 1993. "Work Satisfaction and Stress in the First and Third Year of Academic Appointment." *Journal of Higher Education* 64(4): 453–71.

Olsen, Deborah, Sue A. Maple, and Frances K. Stage. 1995. "Women and Minority Faculty Job Satisfaction." *Journal of Higher Education* 66(3): 267–93.

Olsen, Deborah, and Mary Deane Sorcinelli. 1992. "The Pretenure Years: A Longitudinal Perspective." In *Developing New and Junior Faculty,* edited by Mary Deane Sorcinelli and Ann E. Austin. New Directions for Teaching and Learning No. 50. San Francisco: Jossey-Bass.

Ory, John C., ed. 1989. *Teaching and Its Evaluation: A Handbook of Resources.* Urbana-Champaign: Univ. of Illinois, Office of Instructional Resources.

Ory, John C., and Larry A. Braskamp. 1981. "Faculty Perceptions of the Quality and Usefulness of Three Types of Evaluative Information." *Research in Higher Education* 15(3): 271–82.

Ouchi, William G. 1981. *Theory Z.* New York: Avon Books.

Ouchi, William G., and Alan L. Wilkins. 1985. "Organizational Culture." *Annual Review of Sociology* 11: 457–83.

Overall, J.U., and Herbert W. Marsh. 1979. "Midterm Feedback from Students: Its Relationship to Instructional Improvement and Students' Cognitive and Affective Outcomes." *Journal of Educational Psychology* 71(6): 856–65.

Palmer, James C., and George B. Vaughan, eds. 1992. *Fostering a Climate for Faculty Scholarship at Community Colleges.* Washington, D.C.: American Association of Community and Junior Colleges.

Pambookian, Hagop S. 1976. "Discrepancy between Instructor and Student Evaluation of Instruction: Effect on Instructor." *Instructional Science* 5(1): 63–75.

Parker, Clyde A., and Jane Lawson. March 1978. "From Theory to

Practice to Theory: Consulting with College Faculty." *Personnel and Guidance Journal:* 424–27.

Parsons, Talcott, and Gerald M. Platt. 1973. *The American University.* Cambridge, Mass.: Harvard Univ. Press.

Paulsen, Michael B. 1991. "College Tuition: Demand and Supply Determinants from 1960 –1986." *Review of Higher Education* 14(3): 339–58.

———. 1992. "Building Motivation and Cognition Research into Workshops on Lecturing." *To Improve the Academy* 11: 241–52.

Paulsen, Michael B., and Kenneth A. Feldman. 1995. "Toward a Reconceptualization of Scholarship: A Human Action System with Functional Imperatives." *Journal of Higher Education* 66(6): 615–40.

Perlberg, Arye. 1983. "When Professors Confront Themselves: Towards a Theoretical Conceptualization of Video Self-Confrontation in Higher Education." *Higher Education* 12: 633–63.

Peters, Thomas J., and Robert H. Waterman, Jr. 1982. *In Search of Excellence.* New York: Harper & Row.

Peterson, Marvin W., Kim S. Cameron, Philip Jones, Lisa A. Mets, and Deborah Ettington. 1986. *The Organizational Context for Teaching and Learning.* Ann Arbor, Mich.: National Center for Research to Improve Postsecondary Teaching and Learning.

Peterson, Marvin W., and Melinda G. Spencer. 1990. "Understanding Academic Culture and Climate." In *Assessing Academic Climates and Cultures,* edited by William G. Tierney. New Directions for Institutional Research No. 68. San Francisco: Jossey-Bass.

———. 1993. "Qualitative and Quantitative Approaches to Academic Culture: Do They Tell Us the Same Thing?" In Vol. 9 of *Higher Education: Handbook of Theory and Research,* edited by John C. Smart. New York: Agathon Press.

Pister, Karl S. 1991. "Report of the Universitywide Task Force on Faculty Rewards." Berkeley: Univ. of California.

Povlacs, Joyce T. 1988. "The Teaching Analysis Program and the Role of the Consultant." In *Face to Face: A Sourcebook of Individual Consultation Techniques for Faculty Development Personnel,* edited by Karron G. Lewis and Joyce T. Povlacs. Stillwater, Okla.: New Forums Press.

Quinn, Sandra L., and Sanford B. Kanter. 1984. "Team Teaching: An Alternative to Lecture Fatigue." *Innovation Abstracts* 6(34): 1–2.

Rallis, Helen. 1994. "Creating Teaching and Learning Partnerships with Students: Helping Faculty Listen to Student Voices." *To Improve the Academy* 13: 255–68.

Rando, William C., and Lisa Firing Lenze, eds. 1994. *Learning from Students: Early-Term Student Feedback in Higher Education.* University Park: Pennsylvania State Univ., National Center on Postsecondary Teaching, Learning, and Assessment.

Rando, William C., and Robert J. Menges. 1991. "How Practice Is Shaped by Personal Theories." In *College Teaching: From Theory to Practice.* New Directions for Teaching and Learning No. 45. San Francisco: Jossey-Bass.

Ratcliff, James L., and Associates. 1995. *Realizing the Potential: Improving Postsecondary Teaching, Learning, and Assessment.* University Park: Pennsylvania State Univ., National Center on Postsecondary Teaching, Learning, and Assessment.

Renegar, Sandi, Becky Summary, Charles Bonwell, and James Eison. 1987. "Mandatory Teaching Effectiveness Workshops for New Faculty: Lessons Learned the Hard Way." *Journal of Staff, Program and Organization Development* 5(3): 114–18.

Rhoads, Robert A., and William G. Tierney. 1992. *Cultural Leadership in Higher Education.* University Park: Pennsylvania State Univ., National Center on Postsecondary Teaching, Learning, and Assessment. ED 357 708. 106 pp. MF–01; PC–05.

Rice, Eugene R. Spring 1991. "The New American Scholar: Scholarship and the Purposes of the University." *Metropolitan Universities* 1: 7–18.

Rice, Eugene R., and Ann E. Austin. 1988. "High Faculty Morale." *Change* 20(2): 51–58.

———. 1990. "Organizational Impacts on Faculty Morale and Motivation to Teach." In *How Administrators Can Improve Teaching,* edited by Peter Seldin. San Francisco: Jossey-Bass.

Richardson, Richard C., Jr. 1993. "Creating Effective Learning Environments." In *Faculty as Teachers,* edited by Maryellen Weimer. University Park: Pennsylvania State Univ., National Center on Postsecondary Teaching, Learning, and Assessment.

Richlin, Laurie, ed. 1993. *Preparing Faculty for the New Conceptions of Scholarship.* New Directions for Teaching and Learning No. 54. San Francisco: Jossey-Bass.

Richlin, Laurie, and Brenda Manning. 1995. *Improving a College/University Teaching Evaluation System: A Comprehensive, Developmental Curriculum for Faculty and Administrators.* Pittsburgh: Alliance Publishers.

Riesman, David, and Christopher Jencks. 1962. "The Viability of the

American College." In *The American College,* edited by Nevitt Sanford. New York: John Wiley & Sons.

Rinn, Fauneil J., and Sybil B. Weir. 1984. "Yea, Team." *Improving College and University Teaching* 32(1): 5–10.

Roberts, Alton O., Jon F. Wergin, and Bronwyn E. Adam. 1993. "Institutional Approaches to the Issues of Reward and Scholarship." In *Recognizing Faculty Work: Reward Systems for the Year 2000,* edited by Robert M. Diamond and Bronwyn E. Adam. New Directions for Higher Education No. 81. San Francisco: Jossey-Bass.

Rorschach, Elizabeth, and Robert Whitney. 1986. "Relearning to Teach: Peer Observation as a Means of Professional Development for Teachers." *English Education* 18(3): 159–72.

Rozeman, Judith E., and Michael A. Kerwin. 1991. "Evaluating the Effectiveness of a Teaching Consultation Program on Changing Student Ratings of Teaching Behaviors." *Journal of Staff, Program and Organization Development* 9(4): 223–30.

Rudolph, Frederick. 1990. *The American College and University: A History.* Athens: Univ. of Georgia Press.

Sackmann, Sonja A. 1992. "Culture and Subcultures: An Analysis of Organizational Knowledge." *Administrative Science Quarterly* 37(1): 140–61.

St. John, Edward P. 1994. *Prices, Productivity, and Investment: Assessing Financial Strategies in Higher Education.* ASHE-ERIC Higher Education Report No. 3. Washington, D.C.: George Washington Univ., School of Education and Human Development. ED 382 093. 171 pp. MF–01; PC–07.

Sashkin, Marshall, and Kenneth J. Kiser. 1993. *Putting Total Quality Management to Work: What TQM Means, How to Use It, and How to Sustain It over the Long Run.* San Francisco: Berrett-Koehler Publishers.

Sathe, Vijay. 1983. "Implications of Corporate Culture: A Manager's Guide to Action." *Organizational Dynamics* 12(2): 5–23.

Schein, Edgar H. May 1961. "Management Development as a Process of Influence." *Industrial Management Review (MIT)* 2: 59–77.

———. 1964. "Personal Change through Interpersonal Relationships." In *Interpersonal Dynamics,* edited by W.G. Bennis, E.H. Schein, D.E. Berlew, and F.I. Steele. Belmont, Cal.: Dorsey Press.

———. 1972. *Professional Education.* New York: McGraw-Hill.

———. 1992. *Organizational Culture and Leadership.* San Francisco: Jossey-Bass.

Schein, Edgar H., and Warren G. Bennis. 1965. *Personal and Organizational Change through Group Methods.* New York: John Wiley & Sons.

Schon, Donald A. 1983. *The Reflective Practitioner.* New York: Basic Books.

———. 1987. *Educating the Reflective Practitioner.* San Francisco: Jossey-Bass.

———. 1995. "The New Scholarship Requires a New Epistemology: Knowing in Action." *Change* 27(6): 26–34.

Schuster, Jack H., and Howard R. Bowen. 1985. "The Faculty at Risk." *Change* 17(5): 13–21.

Seagren, Alan T., John W. Creswell, and Daniel W. Wheeler. 1993. *The Department Chair: New Roles, Responsibilities, and Challenges.* ASHE-ERIC Higher Education Report No. 1. Washington, D.C.: George Washington Univ., School of Education and Human Development. ED 363 164. 129 pp. MF–01; PC–06.

Seldin, Peter. 1988. "Evaluating College Teaching." In *College Teaching and Learning: Preparing for New Commitments,* edited by Robert E. Young and Kenneth E. Eble. New Directions for Teaching and Learning No. 33. San Francisco: Jossey-Bass.

———. 1990. *How Administrators Can Improve Teaching.* San Francisco: Jossey-Bass.

———. 1991. *The Teaching Portfolio.* Bolton, Mass.: Anker.

———. 1993. *Successful Use of Teaching Portfolios.* Bolton, Mass.: Anker.

Seldin, Peter, and Linda F. Annis. 1990. "The Teaching Portfolio." *Journal of Staff, Program and Organization Development* 8(4): 197–201.

Seldin, Peter, Linda F. Annis, and John Zubizarreta. 1995. "Using the Teaching Portfolio to Improve Instruction." In *Teaching Improvement Practices,* edited by W. Alan Wright. Bolton, Mass.: Anker.

Sergiovanni, Thomas J. 1992. "Cultural and Competing Perspectives in Administrative Theory and Practice." In *Classics of Organization Theory,* edited by Jay M. Shafritz and J. Steven Ott. Belmont, Cal.: Wadsworth.

Shafritz, Jay M., and J. Steven Ott. 1992. "Organizational Culture and Symbolic Management Organization Theory." In *Classics of Organization Theory,* edited by Jay M. Shafritz and J. Steven Ott. Belmont, Cal.: Wadsworth.

Sharp, Gregory. 1981. "Acquisition of Lecturing Skills by University Teaching Assistants: Some Effects of Interest, Topic Relevance, and Viewing a Model Videotape." *American Educational Research Journal* 18(4): 491–502.

Shatzky, Joel, and Robert Silberman. November 1986. "Master-Students: A Teaching Technique." *JCST:* 119–20.

Shelton, William E., and Deborah DeZure. 1993. "Fostering a Teaching Culture in Higher Education." *Thought and Action: The NEA Higher Education Journal* 8(2): 27–48.

Shore, Bruce M., Stephen F. Foster, Christopher K. Knapper, Gilles G. Nadeau, Neill Neill, and Victor Sim, eds. 1986. *The Teaching Dossier: Its Preparation and Use.* Montreal: Canadian Association of University Teachers.

Showers, Beverly. 1985. "Teachers Coaching Teachers." *Educational Leadership* 42(7): 43–48.

Shulman, Lee S. 1986. "Those Who Understand: Knowledge Growth in Teaching." *Educational Researcher* 15(2): 4–14.

———. 1987. "Knowledge and Teaching: Foundation of the New Reform." *Harvard Educational Review* 57(1): 1–22.

———. 1989. "Toward a Pedagogy of Substance." *AAHE Bulletin* 41(10): 8–13.

———. 1993. "Teaching as Community Property: Putting an End to Pedagogical Solitude." *Change* 25(6): 6–13.

———. 1995. "The Pedagogical Colloquium: Three Models." *AAHE Bulletin* 47(9): 6 –9.

Skoog, Gerald. 1980. "Improving College Teaching through Peer Observation." *Journal of Teacher Education* 31(2): 23 –25.

Smircich, Linda. 1983. "Concepts of Culture and Organizational Analysis." *Administrative Science Quarterly* 28(3): 339–58.

Smith, Myrna J., and Mark LaCelle-Peterson. 1991. "The Professor as Active Learner: Lessons from the New Jersey Master Faculty Program." *To Improve the Academy* 10: 271–78.

Smith, Ron, and Fred Schwartz. 1988. "Improving Teaching by Reflecting on Practice." *To Improve the Academy* 7: 63 –84.

Sorcinelli, Mary Deane. 1984. "An Approach to Colleague Evaluation of Classroom Instruction." *Journal of Instructional Development* 7(4): 11–17.

———. 1988. "Satisfactions and Concerns of New University Teachers." *To Improve the Academy* 7: 121–33.

———. 1992. "New and Junior Faculty Stress: Research and Responses." In *Developing New and Junior Faculty,* edited by Mary Deane Sorcinelli and Ann E. Austin. New Directions for Teaching and Learning No. 50. San Francisco: Jossey-Bass.

———. 1994. "Effective Approaches to New Faculty Development." *Journal of Counseling and Development* 72(5): 474–79.

———. 1995. "How Mentoring Programs Can Improve Teaching."

In *Improving College Teaching,* edited by Peter Seldin. Bolton, Mass.: Anker.

Sorcinelli, Mary Deane, and Ann E. Austin, eds. 1992. *Developing New and Junior Faculty.* New Directions for Teaching and Learning No. 50. San Francisco: Jossey-Bass.

Sorcinelli, Mary Deane, and Janet P. Near. 1989. "Relations between Work and Life away from Work among University Faculty." *Journal of Higher Education* 60(1): 59–81.

Sorenson, D. Lynn. 1994. "Valuing the Student Voice: Student Observer/Consultant Programs." *To Improve the Academy* 13: 97–108.

Stanley, Christine A., and Nancy V. Chism. 1991. "Selected Characteristics of New Faculty: Implications for Faculty Development." *To Improve the Academy* 10: 55–61.

Stevens, Ellen. 1988. "Tinkering with Teaching." *Review of Higher Education* 12(1): 63 –78.

Stevenson, John. 1988. "Evaluating Structured Group Activities for the Large Class." *To Improve the Academy* 7: 39–44.

Sullivan, Arthur M. 1985. "The Role of Two Types of Research on the Evaluation and Improvement of University Teaching." In *Using Research to Improve Teaching,* edited by Janet G. Donald and Arthur M. Sullivan. New Directions for Teaching and Learning No. 23. San Francisco: Jossey-Bass.

Sweeney, John M., and Anthony F. Grasha. February 1979. "Improving Teaching through Faculty Development Triads." *Educational Technology:* 54–57.

Sykes, Charles J. 1988. *ProfScam.* Washington, D.C.: Regnery Gateway.

Tannahill, Andrew, and Graham Robertson. 1986. "Health Education in Medical Education: Collaboration, not Competition." *Medical Teacher* 8(2): 165–70.

Taylor-Way, David. 1988. "Consultation with Video: Memory Management through Stimulated Recall." In *Face to Face: A Sourcebook of Individual Consultation Techniques for Faculty Development Personnel,* edited by Karron G. Lewis and Joyce T. Povlacs. Stillwater, Okla.: New Forums Press.

Taylor-Way, David, and Kathleen T. Brinko. 1989. "Using Video Recall for Improving Professional Competency in Instructional Consultation." *To Improve the Academy* 8: 141–56.

Tiberius, Richard G. 1988. "The Use of the Discussion Group for the Fine-Tuning of Teaching." In *Face to Face: A Sourcebook of Individual Consultation Techniques for Faculty Development*

Personnel, edited by Karron G. Lewis and Joyce T. Povlacs. Stillwater, Okla.: New Forums Press.

—. 1995. "From Shaping Performances to Dynamic Interaction: The Quiet Revolution in Teaching Improvement Programs." In *Teaching Improvement Practices,* edited by W. Alan Wright. Bolton, Mass.: Anker.

Tiberius, Richard G., H. David Sackin, and Lorie Cappe. 1987. "A Comparison of Two Methods for Evaluating Teaching." *Studies in Higher Education* 12(3): 287–97.

Tiberius, Richard G., H. David Sackin, Katharine R. Janzen, and Mary Preece. 1993. "Alliances for Change: A Procedure for Improving Teaching through Conversations with Learners and Partnerships with Colleagues." *Journal of Staff, Program and Organization Development* 11(1): 11–23.

Tiberius, Richard G., H. David Sackin, Joyce M. Slingerland, Kaela Jubas, Mary Bell, and Ann Matlow. 1989. "The Influence of Student Evaluative Feedback on the Improvement of Clinical Teaching." *Journal of Higher Education* 60(6): 665–81.

Tierney, William G. 1988a. "Organizational Culture in Higher Education." *Journal of Higher Education* 59(1): 2–21.

—. 1988b. *The Web of Leadership: The Presidency in Higher Education.* Greenwich, Conn.: JAI Press.

Tierney, William G., and Robert A. Rhoads. 1993. *Enhancing Promotion, Tenure, and Beyond: Faculty Socialization as a Cultural Process.* ASHE-ERIC Higher Education Report No. 6. Washington, D.C.: George Washington Univ., School of Education and Human Development. ED 368 322. 123 pp. MF–01; PC–05.

Tobias, Sheila. March/April 1986. "Peer Perspectives on the Teaching of Science." *Change:* 36–41.

—. 1988. "Peer Perspectives on Physics." *The Physics Teacher* 26(2): 77–80.

Trask, Kerry A. 1989. "The Chairperson and Teaching." In *The Department Chairperson's Role in Enhancing College Teaching,* edited by Ann F. Lucas. New Directions for Teaching and Learning No. 37. San Francisco: Jossey-Bass.

Trice, Harrison M., and Janice M. Beyer. 1984. "Studying Organizational Cultures through Rites and Ceremonials." *Academy of Management Review* 9(4): 653–69.

Tucker, Allan. 1993. *Chairing the Academic Department.* Phoenix: ACE/Oryx Press.

Turner, J.L., and Robert Boice. 1987. "Starting at the Beginning: The

Concerns and Needs of New Faculty." *To Improve the Academy* 6: 41–55.

————. 1989. "Experiences of New Faculty." *Journal of Staff, Program and Organization Development* 7(2): 51–57.

Van Maanen, John. 1978. "People Processing: Strategies of Organizational Socialization." *Organizational Dynamics* 7(1): 19–36.

Van Maanen, John, and Edgar H. Schein. 1979. "Toward a Theory of Organizational Socialization." In Vol. 1 of *Research in Organizational Behavior,* edited by Barry M. Staw. Greenwich, Conn.: JAI Press.

Vaughan, George B., and James C. Palmer, eds. 1991. *Enhancing Teaching and Administration through Scholarship.* New Directions for Community Colleges No. 76. San Francisco: Jossey-Bass.

Vavrus, Linda G., Marilyn L. Grady, and John W. Creswell. 1988. "The Faculty Development Role of Department Chairs: A Naturalistic Analysis." *Planning and Changing* 19(19): 14–29.

Veysey, Lawrence R. 1965. *The Emergence of the American University.* Chicago: Univ. of Chicago Press.

Walker, Charles J. 1991. "Classroom Research in Psychology: Assessment Techniques to Enhance Teaching and Learning." In *Classroom Research: Early Lessons from Success,* edited by Thomas A. Angelo. New Directions for Teaching and Learning No. 46. San Francisco: Jossey-Bass.

Weimer, Maryellen. 1990. *Improving College Teaching.* San Francisco: Jossey-Bass.

————. 1996. "Why Scholarship Is the Bedrock of Good Teaching." In *Teaching on Solid Ground: Using Scholarship to Improve Practice,* edited by Robert J. Menges and Maryellen Weimer. San Francisco: Jossey-Bass.

Weimer, Maryellen, and Lisa Firing Lenze. 1991. "Instructional Interventions: A Review of the Literature on Efforts to Improve Instruction." In Vol. 7 of *Higher Education: Handbook of Theory and Research,* edited by John C. Smart. New York: Agathon.

Welch, Claude, Norman Solkoff, Frank Schimpfhauser, and Norma Henderson. 1988. "The University at Buffalo Program for New Faculty." In *A Handbook for Practitioners,* edited by Emily C. Wadsworth. Professional and Organizational Development Network in Higher Education.

Wergin, Jon F. 1994. *The Collaborative Department.* Washington, D.C.: American Association for Higher Education.

Wheeler, Daniel W. 1992. "The Role of the Chairperson in Support of Junior Faculty." In *Developing New and Junior Faculty,* edited by Mary Deane Sorcinelli and Ann E. Austin. New Directions for Teaching and Learning No. 50. San Francisco: Jossey-Bass.

Wheeler, S. 1966. "The Structure of Formally Organized Socialization Settings." In *Socialization after Childhood,* edited by O.G. Brim and S. Wheeler. New York: John Wiley & Sons.

Whitt, Elizabeth. 1991. "'Hit the Ground Running': Experiences of New Faculty in a School of Education." *Review of Higher Education* 14(2): 177–97.

Wilhite, Myra S. 1990. "Department Heads as Faculty Developers: Six Case Studies." *To Improve the Academy* 9: 111–21.

Wilhite, Myra S., and Anita Leininger. 1988. "Practices Used by Excellent Department Chairs to Enhance the Growth and Development of Faculty." *To Improve the Academy* 7: 189–202.

Wilkins, Alan L. 1983. "The Culture Audit: A Tool for Understanding Organizations." *Organizational Dynamics* 12(2): 24–51.

Williams, Gareth. 1993. "Total Quality Management in Higher Education: Panacea or Placebo?" *Higher Education* 25(3): 229–37.

Wilson, Robert C. 1986. "Improving Faculty Teaching: Effective Use of Student Evaluations and Consultants." *Journal of Higher Education* 57(2): 196–211.

Winkler, Allan M. 1992. "The Faculty Workload Question." *Change* 24(4): 36–41.

Wolverton, Mimi, and Richard C. Richardson, Jr. 1992. "Leadership Strategies to Improve Teaching and Learning." Paper presented at an annual meeting of the Association for the Study of Higher Education, October 29–November 3, Minneapolis, Minnesota. ED 352 914. 28 pp. MF–01; PC–02.

Wright, W. Alan, and M. Carol O'Neil. 1994. "Teaching Improvement Practices: New Perspectives." *To Improve the Academy* 13: 5–37.

———. 1995. "Teaching Improvement Practices: International Perspectives." In *Teaching Improvement Practices,* edited by W. Alan Wright. Bolton, Mass.: Anker.

Wulff, Donald H., Ann Q. Staton-Spicer, Carla W. Hess, and Jody D. Nyquist. 1985. "The Student Perspective on Evaluating Teaching Effectiveness." *ACA Bulletin* 53: 39–47.

INDEX OF SUBJECTS

Cardinal Stritch College in Milwaukee, 118

Carleton professor, 65

Carnegie Foundation innovative reformulation of concept of
 scholarship, 2

Carnegie-Mellon University, University Teaching Center at, 35

Center for Teaching, tasks performed by, 34

central academic administrators emphasize teaching rather than
 research, 3

chair
 importance in instructional improvement, 94–95
 of departments importance in improvement of teaching,
 123–124
 promotion of improved instruction by, 95–99
 steps follow to improve teaching of faculty by, 98

Change, Models of. See instructional improvement, different
 models of

changing as making it happen, 13–15

class interview as way to give feedback to teachers, 59

classroom assessment , 62–63
 reports on successful use for improving instruction, 63

Classroom Student Observer Program, 65

clinical approach to instructional consultation, 60

Clinic to Improve University Teaching at the University of
 Massachusetts, 84

"coaching," use of term of, 69–70

cognitive redefinition and resulting behavioral change, cause of, 14

"collaborative departments," 128

collaborative/process model of consultative interaction 88, 89

colleagues
 as coaches, 67–72
 instructional consultant as, 87–88

college professionals, motivation of, 12

college teachers should become classroom researchers, 4–5

collegial coaching programs
 attributes of effective, 122–123
 classroom visits and observations, 75-77
 colleagues as team teachers,78-83
 common features of, 72
 evaluation of effectiveness by participants, 77-78
 postobservation conference, 77
 preobservation conference, 75
 procedure for selecting participants,74
 training program for collegial coaches,74-75

underlying philosophy of,72-74

colloquia for encouraging collegial interaction and collaboration on
teaching issues, 67

competence, a primary need of novice professor, 102

composition, classroom assessment in, 63

comprehensive model of individual consultation
experimental investigation of effect of, 84-85
feedback value of, 86

confrontational model of consultative interaction, 88

consultants at campus teaching center, background of, 84

consultative interaction, models of, 88–89

"conversation group," 60

"cooperative learning" principles working in the classroom, 82

counselor, instructional consultant as, 87

course material, examination by a collegial coach of, 71–72

criminal justice, classroom assessment in, 63

Cross, K. Patricia, 1, 4

cultural content, deepest level of, 20

culture, forms and substance of, 20

"culture-bearing milieux," 19

"culture of assessment." See supportive teaching culture

culture of teaching, creation of, 19

D

data
stages of comprehensive model of individual consultation,
84
collector, instructional consultant as, 87
manager, instructional consultant as, 87

Department Chair, role of, 93–94

descriptive model for improving instructional effectiveness, 10–11

"descriptive" or "advocacy" research, 132

developmental stages for academic career, 102

diagnostic feedback, need for better , 56

"disconfirmation" clues, 11

"discussion group," 59

"double-loop learning," 42

E

education, classroom assessment in, 63

effective department chairs that support teaching, research on, 67

enhancing subculture, 25

epistemology, questions of, 129

"generic view" of the academic career, 102
Georgetown University, 32
good teaching as a necessary but not sufficient condition for
        tenure, 37
group discussion as way to give feedback to teachers, 59
group interviews
        and written comments more accurate for improving
        instruction, 58
        at midterm preferred by students over standardized ratings
        at end of term, 58

H

hierarchical team, 80
highest faculty income and research, positive association between, 2
human relations training, studies of, 11
human systems, general theory of change in, 11

I

identification
        mechanism, 14
        stage of instructional change, 66
improvement strategy stage of comprehensive model of individual
        consultation, 84
Indiana University, 72
individual consultations, stages in comprehensive model of, 84
Informal socialization, 110
information source, instructional consultant as, 87
informative feedback. See also formative evaluation
        practice-centered inquiry for, 40–46
        that motivates professors, 40
instructional consultants, roles of, 86–88
instructional consultation
        comprehensive process of, 83–86
        models of, 83, 123
instructional developers, need to draw upon extensive experience
        of, 6
instructional feedback, definition of , 89. See also feedback
instructional improvement
        different models of, 9–11
        from a faculty perspective, 9
        support for, 2–3
"instructional paradigm," absence of emphasis on learning in ,
        129–130

instructional productivity
> associated with increase in quality of student learning experiences, 4
> deceptive gains in, 3

interactive model of team teaching, reports of successful experiences with, 81–82

interactive team, 81

intrinsic motivation theory, 12

J

"job characteristics model," 12

L

learner control of adult learner, 68

learning, types one might want to assess , 63

lecture, most common approach to teaching among new faculty, 104

Lewin, general theory of change in human systems of , 11

Lilly Endowment Teaching Fellows Program, 33, 115–116
> evaluative study of, 29
> evaluation of, 94

Luther College in Iowa, 114–115

M

McGill University, 45, 48

management development, studies of, 11

mathematics, classroom assessment in, 63

meaningful gains in instructional productivity requirement, 4

meaningfulness of work depends upon three characteristics of job, 12

Mentoring as component of Teaching Fellows Program, 118

mentoring programs
> detailed and comprehensive two-year study of, 119–120
> for new faculty, 115–120

Miami-Dade Community College's Teaching and Learning Project receives award, 30

Miami University's Teaching Scholars Program, 117–118

"moment of truth," as point at which the consultant gives feedback to the instructor, 90

Myers-Briggs Type Indicator for personality assessments, 119

N

new behavior, mechanisms for sustaining, 15

New England College of Optometry, 80, 80–81
New Jersey Institute for Collegiate Teaching and Learning, 72
New Jersey Master Faculty Program, 72–74
New York University, 72
nursing, classroom assessment in, 63

O

Ohio State University, 44
Oklahoma Junior College, 72
"one-minute paper," 62
opportunities for
      research on interaction and collaboration between
      colleagues on teaching, 67
      " to talk about teaching" in supportive teaching culture, 33
organizational
      contribution of cultural perspective on behavior, 19–20
      change, studies of, 11
      culture, concepts of, 19–22
organizations as "culture-bearing milieux," 19
orientation
      and mentoring perceived value in instructional
      improvement,111
      as need for better information at start of the year, 111–112
      methods for new faculty, 112–113
      that focused on basic teaching skills for college instructors,
      112
      workshops value for new faculty, 109
orthogonal subculture, 25

P

Parsonian four-function paradigm, 27
part-time faculty, programs to help, 127
pedagogical colloquium model, 32
pedagogical practices, gaps in research on, 131–132
Pennsylvania State University, 61
personal autonomy of adult learner, 68
physical education, classroom assessment in, 63
physics, classroom assessment in, 63
political science, classroom assessment in, 63
"practice-centered behavior," 42
practice-centered inquiry, 40–46
"practice of research" elevated into an all-encompassing ideal, 23
prescription model of consultative interaction, 88

---

pretenure years, reasons why stressful time , 103
product model of consultative interaction, 88
Professional and Organizational Network in Higher Education, 44
profile similarity, 47
ProfScam, 3
psychology, 63, 95-96

Q

Quality,
 concern about, 1–4
 control circles as way to give feedback to teachers, 59
 gain of student learning experiences increases instructional productivity, 4

R

reactive tinkerers, 46
"reflective conversation with the situation," 42
reflective practice as way of expanding strategies for improving instruction, 67
"reflective practitioners"
 teacher as, 49
 college professors as, 41, 125, 133
The Reflective Practitioner (1983), epistemology of practice presented by, 4
reflective tinkerers, 46
Refreezing, 15–16
report, purpose of this, 6–7
"research surge" intensification in the past decade, 23
role models and socialization, 110
"RSQC2" starter technique in classroom assessment, 62–63

S

scanning, mechanism of, 14
scanning stage of instructional change, 66
Schein, studies of , 11
scholarship
 concept, Carnegie Foundation innovative reformulation of, 2
 equals research, challenge to view that, 31
 new forms of, 129
Scholarship Reconsidered report, 2
Schon, Donald, 4
Self-Assessment

ASHE-ERIC HIGHER EDUCATION REPORTS

Since 1983, the Association for the Study of Higher Education (ASHE) and the Educational Resources Information Center (ERIC) Clearinghouse on Higher Education, a sponsored project of the Graduate School of Education and Human Development at The George Washington University, have cosponsored the ASHE-ERIC Higher Education Report series. The 1995 series is the 24th overall and the seventh to be published by the Graduate School of Education and Human Development at The George Washington University.

Each monograph is the definitive analysis of a tough higher education problem, based on thorough research of pertinent literature and institutional experiences. Topics are identified by a national survey. Noted practitioners and scholars are then commissioned to write the reports, with experts providing critical reviews of each manuscript before publication.

Eight monographs (10 before 1985) in the ASHE-ERIC Higher Education Report series are published each year and are available on individual and subscription bases. To order, use the order form on the last page of this book.

Qualified persons interested in writing a monograph for the ASHE-ERIC Higher Education Reports are invited to submit a proposal to the National Advisory Board. As the pre-eminent literature review and issue analysis series in higher education, we can guarantee wide dissemination and national exposure for accepted candidates. Execution of a monograph requires at least a minimal familiarity with the ERIC database, including *Resources in Education* and current *Index to Journals in Education.* The objective of these reports is to bridge conventional wisdom with practical research. Prospective authors are strongly encouraged to call Dr. Fife at 800-773-3742.

For further information, write to

ASHE-ERIC Higher Education Reports
The George Washington University
One Dupont Circle, Suite 630
Washington, DC 20036

Or phone (202) 296-2597; toll free: 800-773-ERIC.

Write or call for a complete catalog.

ADVISORY BOARD

Barbara E. Brittingham
University of Rhode Island

Mildred Garcia
Montclair State College

Rodolfo Z. Garcia
North Central Association of Colleges and Schools

James Hearn
University of Georgia

Bruce Anthony Jones
University of Pittsburgh

L. Jackson Newell
Deep Springs College

Carolyn Thompson
State University of New York–Buffalo

CONSULTING EDITORS

Marsha B. Baxter Magolda
Miami University

E. Grady Bogue
The University of Tennessee

Robert Boice
State University of New York at Stony Brook

John M. Braxton
Vanderbilt University

Kate Brinko
Appalachian State University

John A. Centra
Syracuse University

Robert A. Cornesky
Cornesky and Associates, Inc.

Peter Ewell
National Center for Higher Education Management Systems

John Folger
Institute for Public Policy Studies

Leonard Goldberg
University of Richmond

George Gordon
University of Strathclyde

Jane Halonen
Alverno College

Dean L. Hubbard
Northwest Missouri State University

Thomas F. Kelley
Binghamton University

Daniel T. Layzell
University of Wisconsin System

Robert Menges
Northwestern University

Keith Miser
Colorado State University

L. Jackson Newell
University of Utah

James Rhem
The National Teaching & Learning Forum

Gary Rhoades
University of Arizona

G. Jeremiah Ryan
Harford Community College

Karl Schilling
Miami University

Charles Schroeder
University of Missouri

Lawrence A. Sherr
University of Kansas

Patricia A. Spencer
Riverside Community College

Marilla D. Svinicki
University of Texas at Austin

David Sweet
OERI, U.S. Department of Education

Barbara E. Taylor
Association of Governing Boards

Wesley K. Willmer
Biola University

Donald H. Wulff
University of Washington

Manta Yorke
Liverpool John Moores University

REVIEW PANEL

Charles Adams
University of Massachusetts at Amherst

Louis Albert
American Association for Higher Education

Richard Alfred
University of Michigan

Henry Lee Allen
University of Rochester

Philip G. Altbach
Boston College

Marilyn J. Amey
University of Kansas

Kristine L. Anderson
Florida Atlantic University

Karen D. Arnold
Boston College

Robert J. Barak
Iowa State Board of Regents

Alan Bayer
Virginia Polytechnic Institute and State University

John P. Bean
Indiana University–Bloomington

John M. Braxton
Peabody College, Vanderbilt University

Ellen M. Brier
Tennessee State University

Barbara E. Brittingham
The University of Rhode Island

Dennis Brown
University of Kansas

Peter McE. Buchanan
Council for Advancement and Support of Education

Patricia Carter
University of Michigan

John A. Centra
Syracuse University

Arthur W. Chickering
George Mason University

Darrel A. Clowes
Virginia Polytechnic Institute and State University

Cynthia S. Dickens
Mississippi State University

Deborah M. DiCroce
Piedmont Virginia Community College

Sarah M. Dinham
University of Arizona

Kenneth A. Feldman
State University of New York at Stony Brook

Dorothy E. Finnegan
The College of William & Mary

Mildred Garcia
Montclair State College

Rodolfo Z. Garcia
Commission on Institutions of Higher Education

Kenneth C. Green
University of Southern California

James Hearn
University of Georgia

Edward R. Hines
Illinois State University

Deborah Hunter
University of Vermont

Philo Hutcheson
Georgia State University

Bruce Anthony Jones
University of Pittsburgh

Elizabeth A. Jones
The Pennsylvania State University

Kathryn Kretschmer
University of Kansas

Marsha V. Krotseng
State College and University Systems of West Virginia

George D. Kuh
Indiana University–Bloomington

Daniel T. Layzell
University of Wisconsin System

Patrick G. Love
Kent State University

Cheryl D. Lovell
State Higher Education Executive Officers

Meredith Jane Ludwig
American Association of State Colleges and Universities

Dewayne Matthews
Western Interstate Commission for Higher Education

Mantha V. Mehallis
Florida Atlantic University

Toby Milton
Essex Community College

James R. Mingle
State Higher Education Executive Officers

John A. Muffo
Virginia Polytechnic Institute and State University

L. Jackson Newell
Deep Springs College

James C. Palmer
Illinois State University

Robert A. Rhoads
The Pennsylvania State University

G. Jeremiah Ryan
Harford Community College

Mary Ann Danowitz Sagaria
The Ohio State University

Daryl G. Smith
The Claremont Graduate School

William G. Tierney
University of Southern California

Susan B. Twombly
University of Kansas

Robert A. Walhaus
University of Illinois–Chicago

Harold Wechsler
University of Rochester

Elizabeth J. Whitt
University of Illinois–Chicago

Michael J. Worth
The George Washington University

RECENT TITLES

1995 ASHE-ERIC Higher Education Reports

1. Tenure, Promotion and Reappointment: Legal and Administrative Implications
   Benjamin Baez and John Centra

1994 ASHE-ERIC Higher Education Reports

1. The Advisory Committee Advantage: Creating an Effective Strategy for Programmatic Improvement
   Lee Teitel

2. Collaborative Peer Review: The Role of Faculty in Improving College Teaching
   Larry Keig and Michael D. Waggoner

3. Prices, Productivity, and Investment: Assessing Financial Strategies in Higher Education
   Edward P. St. John

4. The Development Officer in Higher Education: Toward an Understanding of the Role
   Michael J. Worth and James W. Asp II

5. The Promises and Pitfalls of Performance Indicators in Higher Education
   Gerald Gaither, Brian P. Nedwek, and John E. Neal

6. A New Alliance: Continuous Quality and Classroom Effectiveness
   Mimi Wolverton

7. Redesigning Higher Education: Producing Dramatic Gains in Student Learning
   Lion F. Gardiner

8. Student Learning Outside the Classroom: Transcending Artificial Boundaries
   George D. Kuh, Katie Branch Douglas, Jon P. Lund, and Jackie Ramin-Gyurnek

1993 ASHE-ERIC Higher Education Reports

1. The Department Chair: New Roles, Responsibilities, and Challenges
   Alan T. Seagren, John W. Creswell, and Daniel W. Wheeler

2. Sexual Harassment in Higher Education: From Conflict to Community
   Robert O. Riggs, Patricia H. Marred, and JoAnn C. Cutting

3. Chicanos in Higher Education: Issues and Dilemmas for the 21st Century
   Adalberto Aguirre Jr., and Ruben O. Martinez

4. Academic Freedom in American Higher Education: Rights, Responsibilities, and Limitations
   Robert K. Posh

5. Making Sense of the Dollars: The Costs and Uses of Faculty Compensation
   Kathryn M. Moore and Marilyn J. Amey

6. Enhancing Promotion, Tenure and Beyond: Faculty Socialization as a Cultural Process
   William C. Tierney and Robert A. Rhoads

7. New Perspectives for Student Affairs Professionals: Evolving Realities, Responsibilities, and Roles
   Peter H. Garland and Thomas W. Grace

8. Turning Teaching into Learning: The Role of Student Responsibility in the Collegiate Experience
   Todd M. Davis and Patricia Hillman Murrell

1992 ASHE-ERIC Higher Education Reports

1. The Leadership Compass: Values and Ethics in Higher Education
   John R. Wilcox and Susan L. Ebbs

2. Preparing for a Global Community: Achieving an International Perspective in Higher Education
   Sarah M. Pickert

3. Quality: Transforming Postsecondary Education
   Ellen Earle Chaffee and Lawrence A. Sherr

4. Faculty Job Satisfaction: Women and Minorities in Peril
   Martha Wingard Tack and Carol Logan Patitu

5. Reconciling Rights and Responsibilities of Colleges and Students: Offensive Speech, Assembly, Drug Testing, and Safety
   Annette Gibbs

6. Creating Distinctiveness: Lessons from Uncommon Colleges and Universities
   Barbara K. Townsend, L. Jackson Newell, and Michael D. Wiese

7. Instituting Enduring Innovations: Achieving Continuity of Change in Higher Education
   Barbara K. Curry

8. Crossing Pedagogical Oceans: International Teaching Assistants in U.S. Undergraduate Education
   Rosslyn M. Smith, Patricia Byrd, Gayle L. Nelson, Ralph Pat Barrett, and Janet C. Constantinides

1991 ASHE-ERIC Higher Education Reports

1. Active Learning: Creating Excitement in the Classroom
   Charles C. Bonwell and James A. Eison

2. Realizing Gender Equality in Higher Education: The Need to Integrate Work/Family Issues
   Nancy Hensel

3. Academic Advising for Student Success: A System of Shared
Responsibility
   Susan H. Frost

4. Cooperative Learning: Increasing College Faculty Instructional
Productivity
   David W. Johnson, Roger T. Johnson, and Karl A. Smith

5. High School–College Partnerships: Conceptual Models,
Programs, and Issues
   Arthur Richard Greenberg

6. Meeting the Mandate: Renewing the College and
Departmental Curriculum
   William Toombs and William Tierney

7. Faculty Collaboration: Enhancing the Quality of Scholarship
and Teaching
   Ann E. Austin and Roger G. Baldwin

8. Strategies and Consequences: Managing the Costs in Higher
Education
   John S. Waggaman

1990 ASHE-ERIC Higher Education Reports

1. The Campus Green: Fund Raising in Higher Education
   Barbara E. Brittingham and Thomas R. Pezzullo

2. The Emeritus Professor: Old Rank, New Meaning
   James E. Mauch, Jack W. Birch, and Jack Matthews

3. "High Risk" Students in Higher Education: Future Trends
   Dionne J. Jones and Betty Collier Watson

4. Budgeting for Higher Education at the State Level: Enigma,
Paradox, and Ritual
   Daniel T. Layzell and Jan W. Lyddon

5. Proprietary Schools: Programs, Policies, and Prospects
   John B. Lee and Jamie P. Merisotis

6. College Choice: Understanding Student Enrollment Behavior
   Michael B. Paulsen

7. Pursuing Diversity: Recruiting College Minority Students
   Barbara Astone and Elsa Nuñez-Wormack

8. Social Consciousness and Career Awareness: Emerging Link
in Higher Education
   John S. Swift Jr.

ORDER FORM

Quantity   **Amount**

_____ Please begin my subscription to the 1995 *ASHE-ERIC Higher Education Reports* at $98.00, 31% off the cover price, starting with Report 1, 1995. Includes shipping. _____

_____ Please send a complete set of the 1994 *ASHE-ERIC Higher Education Reports* at $98.00, 31% off the cover price. Please add shipping charge below. _____

Individual reports are available at the following prices:
1993, 1994, and 1995, $18.00; 1988–1992, $17.00; 1980–1987, $15.00

SHIPPING CHARGES
For orders of more than 50 books, please call for shipping information.

	1st three books	Ea. addl. book
U.S., 48 Contiguous States		
Ground:	$3.75	$0.15
2nd Day*:	8.25	1.10
Next Day*:	18.00	1.60
Alaska & Hawaii (2nd Day Only)*:	13.25	1.40

U.S. Territories and Foreign Countries: Please call for shipping information.
*Order will be shipped within 24 hours of request.
All prices shown on this form are subject to change.

PLEASE SEND ME THE FOLLOWING REPORTS:

Quantity	Report No.	Year	Title	Amount

Please check one of the following:

☐ Check enclosed, payable to GWU-ERIC.
☐ Purchase order attached ($45.00 minimum).
☐ Charge my credit card indicated below:
    ☐ Visa   ☐ MasterCard

Subtotal: _____

Shipping: _____

Total Due: _____

Expiration Date_____

Name_____

Title_____

Institution _____

Address_____

City _____ State _____ Zip_____

Phone _____ Fax _____ Telex_____

Signature _____ Date_____

SEND ALL ORDERS TO: ASHE-ERIC Higher Education Reports
The George Washington University
One Dupont Cir., Ste. 630, Washington, DC 20036-1183
Phone: (202) 296-2597 • Toll-free: 800-773-ERIC